# CLASSIC ANCIENT
# MYTHOLOGY

# CLASSIC ANCIENT MYTHOLOGY

Richard Patrick   Peter Croft

This edition published 1987 by
Cathay Books
59 Grosvenor Street, London W1

© 1972, 1974, 1978, 1987 Hennerwood Publications Limited

ISBN 0 86178 493 6

Produced by Mandarin Publishers Limited
22a Westlands Road
Quarry Bay, Hong Kong
Printed in Hong Kong

# CONTENTS

# Egyptian Mythology

# INTRODUCTION

The history of ancient Egyptian civilization falls, by the convention of modern historians, into three main periods or phases: the Old Kingdom, or Pyramid Age; the Middle Kingdom, sometimes misleadingly called the Feudal Age; and the New Kingdom, when Egypt became an imperial power and reached the apex of her prosperity and influence. These 'Kingdoms', however, are no more than landmarks or peak periods in what was in reality a continuous process of political and cultural development lasting through almost three thousand years of pharanoic rule. The roots of Egyptian civilization lay deep in her past, before written records began and before the country became a single kingdom united under one rule. They can be dimly glimpsed in the simple material remains of the prehistoric period – the designs on pots found in the graves, the decoration on stone palettes for grinding eyepaint or on ivory combs and knife-handles. Memories of an earlier age also survive in religious literature, in the very ancient texts inscribed in some of the Old Kingdom pyramids, and in ritual practices and the insignia and paraphernalia of royal and temple panoply. Most important of all was the continuing dual nature of Egyptian kingship.

Symmetry and balance were characteristic both of the art and the literature of ancient Egypt, and many heraldic groups of opposing figures symbolized North and South, East and West, Good and Evil, the cultivated land and the desert, Egypt and non-Egypt (i.e. the rest of mankind). In the legends, Truth did battle with Falsehood, Horus the god of fertile Egypt with Seth, the red god of deserts. Above all, Egypt itself was a double kingdom; its pharaoh was 'Lord of the Two Lands', and 'King of Upper and Lower Egypt.' The south, or Upper Egypt, was the narrow strip of cultivated earth on either side of the Nile, sometimes only a few miles wide, which stretched from the cataract at Aswan to the ancient capital Memphis, near modern Cairo. Lower Egypt was the wide alluvial Delta, its waterways spreading fanlike from the apex near Memphis and Heliopolis towards the two hundred mile long coastline of the Mediterranean. In popular memory these Two Lands were once separate, but had been united by a certain Menes, who was thought to have been the first king of the First Dynasty. Thenceforward the memory of the unification was preserved in the titles and insignia of the King and some officials. The king wore a double crown, the Red Crown of the Delta being combined with the white mitre of Upper Egypt; on his throne the heraldic plants symbolic of North and South were entwined, and on his forehead he sometimes wore twin diadems, the symbols of the vulture-goddess Nekhebet of Upper

Egypt and the cobra-goddess Buto of the Delta. The king's coronation rites were performed in duplicate, once for the north, and once for the south. By temperament and in their way of life the dwellers of Upper Egypt were different from those of the Delta, and they spoke a different dialect as they do to this day. Their cult practices and beliefs were therefore very different and many of their myths had a strongly local flavour.

Modern archaeological discovery in the various countries of the Levant has given the lie to the old belief that the valley of the Nile was the cradle of civilization, and that everything began in Egypt. We know nowadays that most of the important discoveries which were landmarks in the early progress of mankind occurred elsewhere, in the hills of Palestine and Syria, the alluvial plain of Mesopotamia or the uplands of Persia and Anatolia, and sometimes even further afield. Thus the Egyptians were not, so far as we can see, the first agriculturalists, nor were they the first potters, nor the first workers in metal. Moreover the idea of writing – that essential invention without which man cannot convey his ideas and develop an urban society – probably reached Egypt from some neighbouring country. Nevertheless, the brilliant use to which the Egyptians put these newly-learned skills soon placed them in the forefront of ancient civilizations. Because of their relative isolation, and the unique nature of their way of life, Egyptian civilization developed a highly individual character which was the wonder and admiration of most of their neighbours.

The Greeks recognized the uniqueness of Egypt. The historian Herodotus, who visited the Nile valley in the fifth century BC, was filled with astonishment with what he saw and wrote as follows: – 'Just as the Egyptians have a climate peculiar to themselves, and their river is different in its nature from all other rivers, so they have made themselves customs and laws of a kind contrary to those of all other men.' Of the native customs he describes, none were more strange in his eyes or more different from Greek religious practice than the cults of the various gods and goddesses and their animal counterparts. These rites and beliefs he found everywhere, and concluded that the Egyptians 'were beyond measure religious, more than any other nation'.

It is probably true to say that among no other ancient people were the strands of belief in the supernatural so closely interwoven with their daily lives, their personal relationships, their hopes and fears, and their attitude to authority. The day-to-day hazards of existence were the work of hostile powers; scorpions and snakes could be warded off by amulets worn on the body, or incantations written on scrolls and kept in the house. In times of hazard such as childbirth and illness the deities of the hearth and home were invoked, and Bes, the domestic god who watched over sleep, was carved on the bed and walls. Sowing and harvest were times when offerings must be made to the gods

who gave success to these operations, and the River Nile, itself a god, must be placated lest he rise too swiftly or be too niggardly with his life-giving waters.

Besides these potentially hostile or friendly spirits of the house and field and threshing-floor, there were greater deities who represented the various forces of nature. In the early days, local tribal gods in the various regions of the country had been embodiments of different aspects of nature. Then some villages grew into towns or cities, while others became grouped into districts, and districts into political units (for administrative purposes, the so called 'nomes'), and the city- or nome-gods grew in importance until some were so widely worshipped that they became national gods. Thus the growth of the pantheon reflects the political growth of Egypt from its tribal origins in predynastic times. Similarly the introduction into the pantheon of newcomers reflects the influx of foreigners or of foreign influences either at times of weakness when the country was subject to immigration, or in times of strength when she controlled an empire abroad.

In the Old Kingdom, about 2600 BC, early Egyptian civilization reached a very high level. The whole country was efficiently organized under the centralized control of the royal family and power and wealth were concentrated at court. Craftsmen and architects, quarrymen and masons worked for the king and the small circle of officials surrounding him, many of whom were royal princes. Temples were erected to the great gods; Ptah the god of the capital, Memphis, Ra the god of Heliopolis from whom the king claimed descent, Hathor the great goddess of Dendera, and Horus whose incarnation the king was thought to be. However the resources of the country, in manpower and materials, were lavished in greatest measure on the building of huge pyramid tombs for the kings themselves, on costly burial places for their relatives and dependents, and on the endowment of priesthoods which were to carry on for ever the funerary cult of the dead. All these were non-productive ends which dissipated the country's wealth. Bankruptcy, the breakdown of central control and the dissipation of power into the hands of the nobles led to anarchy and civil war and for a time disrupted the realm. Asiatic Bedouin, in the confusion, poured into the Delta, while tribesmen from Nubia overran Upper Egypt, and art declined and trade dwindled.

Shortly before 2000 BC, the country was reunited by a Theban family of warrior-kings, whose energy and competence restored order and inaugurated the Middle Kingdom (about 2050–1780 BC). The Thebans had started their career as nomarchs (that is, rulers of their local nome), and they had gained the ascendancy with the help of other nomarchs almost equally powerful. These nobles continued to wield considerable influence under

the crown, and lived in their own domains in almost royal style; their palaces were miniature courts, they could command the work of craftsmen and artists, and some of the finest works of art of the Middle Kingdom came not from the capital, but from the nomes. Cults of local gods such as Sobek of the Faiyum, Min of Coptos and Amon of Thebes flourished.

The Middle Kingdom was followed by a second period of weakness and confusion from which few material remains have survived. Foreigners from nearby Palestine poured into the Delta and for a time controlled virtually the whole country; they were finally expelled, after bitter conflict, by another Theban family whose triumph ushered in the most glorious era of Egypt's history, the New Kingdom (*circa* 1570-1085 BC). Now the armies of Pharaoh, experienced in warfare, set about the conquest of Palestine. Fortresses secured the eastern and western borders of the Delta against possible attack, and then the Egyptians marched north till they reached the River Euphrates in Syria, not far from the present Turkish border. In the south, the Sudan as far as the fourth cataract was brought under Egyptian control and the gold mines of Nubia were exploited to the full.

Egypt was now the wealthiest country in the world. Corn and cattle, timber and precious metals, incense, wine and oil, the tribute of the empire, poured into her treasuries, and emissaries from distant potentates brought the riches of Mesopotamia, Anatolia and the Aegean as diplomatic gifts. The gods were the chief beneficiaries of this wealth, and especially the King's family god Amon, who as Amon-Ra became the state god. Huge temples were built for him, the elegant temple of Luxor and the large and elaborate temple at Karnak. Added to by successive kings, this great metropolitan shrine received its most imposing addition in the mighty pillared hall built by Seti I about 1310 BC and then was completed by his son Rameses II, sometimes called Rameses the Great. This remarkable man, during his long reign of sixty seven years, carried out a stupendous building programme not only in every cult centre of Egypt but also in Nubia, where he dedicated no less than seven temples to the local gods and the great gods. In these temples he is depicted as a god himself and on the facade of the largest, the rock-temple of Abu Simbel, (now rescued from the rising waters of the High Dam by a spectacular feat of modern engineering), four colossal seated statues of the king, nearly seventy feet high, dwarf even the figures of the gods themselves.

Rameses' battle with the Hittites, which is the theme of the reliefs on several of his temples, was virtually Egypt's last imperial encounter. Seventy years later she had lost virtually all her possessions and was even threatened with invasion; though the danger was averted the New Kingdom declined in prosperity and in authority; the administration became corrupt and civil war weakened the throne. In the so-called Late Period, the rule of successive dynasties of foreigners – Libyans, negroes from the

Sudan, Assyrians and finally Persians left Egypt totally bereft of inspiration and struggling vainly against crippling taxation and military occupation.

Persian rule in Egypt ended in 332 BC with the arrival of the Macedonian, Alexander the Great. Though he stayed only a short time in Egypt, he was welcomed as a deliverer and paid homage to the gods. After his death the country was organized as a province of the empire and one of Alexander's generals, Ptolemy, was put in charge. Finally in 305 BC he was crowned king of Egypt, as Ptolemy the Saviour. He was the first of a long dynasty of Ptolemies, the last of whom was the son of Cleopatra. Under the Ptolemaic dynasty large numbers of Greek settlers made the country their home and Greek towns sprang up. The greatest of these was Alexandria, founded by Alexander himself on the Mediterranean coast, which rapidly became the greatest city in the Hellenistic world. But although Egypt was now run by foreigners, and Greek was the official language, the native population were allowed to keep their ancient customs and to practise their religion, and the Ptolemies were careful to pay court to the ancient gods, adopting the titles and insignia of Pharaohs, and themselves performing the necessary rites. Much of the information we possess about Egyptian mythology and ritual comes from the huge temples which the Ptolemies built or began to build, and which were completed and further embellished by the Romans who in 30 BC took over the country. The Caesars, like the Ptolemies, are shown on the walls of these temples worshipping the gods of Egypt, but few of them visited the country or knew anything of its traditions. Many Egyptian deities, however, acquired new forms under Hellenistic and Roman rule and the cult of some, such as Isis and Serapis, spread to the farthest ends of the Roman Empire.

Descriptions of life in ancient Egypt have survived in detail and as the climate of Egypt is one of the best in the world, life for all free men was pleasant enough, it would seem. The Egyptian village of the New Kingdom must have been very like the villages of today. Houses were built of unbaked brick, as they are still, and had usually several rooms and steps up to the flat roof on which, in the heat of summer, the family could sleep. Houses of the well-to-do usually had more than one storey and were surrounded by a garden full of palm and acacia trees; in it there was usually a pool on which lotus flowers bloomed and ducks swam. Medium-sized houses had a small walled garden with one or two shady trees and frequently a verandah or porch. Furniture consisted of beds, chairs or stools, and low tables; boxes held clothes, cosmetic articles and other possessions, and wooden stands supported wine jars and large water pots. Mats, woven hangings and flower vases adorned the rooms and the plastered walls were usually painted. The most luxurious houses had a kind of air-conditioning in the form of vents conducting cool air down from the roof and the kitchens and servants' quarters in these luxury villas were often in a separate building.

The Egyptians enjoyed parties and are shown seated at banquets, men and women together, tended by maids who filled the wine bowls and distributed lotus blossoms and perfumed oil to the guests, while musicians played and danced or acrobats tumbled. Pastimes for the wealthy were board games resembling trictrac or ludo, fishing with harpoon or net, and fowling with throwsticks in the marshy papyrus thickets which abounded in wild birds. On hunting expeditions in the desert with their hounds they found ample game, including several species of antelope and gazelle, wild cattle, and that most royal prey, the lion.

Such were the occupations of a busy official during his hours of ease. The peasant or *fellah* had little leisure, if we are to judge by the scenes carved and painted in the tombs of their masters, who are shown inspecting the daily work of their servants and serfs on their estates. Agriculture depended on the river Nile, which flooded its banks with predictable regularity, covering the fields as far as the desert edge. The floodwaters soaked into the earth and when after some weeks they subsided the soil, fertilised by a fresh deposit of silt, was soon dry enough for ploughing. Wheat and barley were the main crops and instead of the cotton of today, flax provided fibres for the manufacture of linen, the universal textile.

Egypt was a totalitarian state; the king's word was the law and legislation was by royal edict. The King was a being apart from all other mortals. His upbringing included instruction in all sports and military accomplishments. By tradition he was braver, wiser and more physically powerful than any of his subjects; none could bend his bow and none shoot so far and so straight. For Pharaoh (the word means 'Great House' and was used in the Late Period to refer, obliquely and respectfully, to the lord of the palace) was a god, a being apart from all mortals; he was deemed to be the child of the sun-god Ra, begotten by Amon-Ra himself who had taken the form of the reigning king at the time of his conception. Khnum the creator-god was thought to have fashioned him in the womb of the queen-mother, and when he was born, the divine child was suckled by wise goddesses. When he succeeded to the throne, he was solemnly crowned by priests dressed as gods, and after thirty years on the throne, further rites revived his waning powers and confirmed his supremacy. The country's well-being depended on him, and it was believed that without his continuing presence, cosmic order would be overthrown, the Nile would cease to flood, and famine and disaster overtake Egypt.

The most admired of professions was that of the scribe. The

tools of their trade were their pencase often inscribed with their name, their ink pot and brushes and their rolls of papyrus. A scribe's apprenticeship was long; he had to learn to draw, in the correct form, some seven hundred hieroglyphic or picture signs and also their hieratic equivalents (the hieroglyphs were carved in stone; hieratic was the simplified form of the signs devised for rapid writing in ink on papyrus or on potsherd or limestone flakes). The word 'hieroglyph' means 'Sacred Writing' and the scribe regarded his calling seriously and before embarking on some new scroll, would pour a libation to Thoth, the god of writing.

Because of its sacred character, the script was conservative. Each pictorial sign was drawn in a way hallowed by custom since its inception and virtually unchanged through three thousand years. Essentially, the system was a simple one. A picture or ideogram represented each word, and then determinatives, denoting action, and homophones, denoting abstracts, were added to each principle sign. Hieroglyphs were written in continuous lines and were not divided by punctuation into words or sentences. Their essentially pictorial character made them very decorative, and often little details such as the feathers of a bird's wing, or the mottled skin of a snake are carved with great care on the stone. The magical nature of hieroglyphic writing was never entirely lost sight of, and sometimes a sign representing a dangerous creature such as a crocodile or snake would have been rendered harmless by severing the head or transfixing it with a knife or harpoon. Towards the end of the pharaonic period in the first millennium BC, the hieroglyphic system became more complicated and augmented by a number of new signs until in the Ptolemaic period, thousands of signs are found on the temple walls where the priestly scribes exercised their ingenuity in the invention of cryptographic writings that only they could read, thus nullifying the function for which written communication was invented. The last surviving hieroglyphic inscription is dated 395 AD, in the reign of the Roman emperor Theodosius.

The Afterlife was of great importance to the ancient Egyptians and few people have devoted so much of their time and wealth to preparation for their death than they did. From the moment of his accession, a king started to plan and to build his tomb and the funerary temple attached to it, where his cult was to be perpetuated after his death. The wealth of officials and commoners, to a lesser degree, was also hoarded to provide suitable funerary equipment, the costly rite of mummification whereby the body was preserved, and the elaborate and costly funeral itself which might involve hundreds of participants, both priests and laymen. The afterlife was conceived of as continuation of life on earth and so the dead man would need, in his tomb, all those necessities and luxuries which made life on this earth pleasant. At the same time, the Egyptians were a realistic people and they had a very human fear of death; its inevitability was always before them.

How then did they reconcile the inevitable fact of death with the divinity of their king who, as a god, must be above death? The answer was to be found in the myth of the god Osiris who was believed once to have ruled Egypt as king. He was murdered by his brother Set, who seized the throne but was at last defeated by Osiris' son Horus; he avenged his father and became in turn king of Egypt. Osiris, the embodiment of vegetation which dies in winter and is resurrected in spring, lived on as lord of the Underworld and every king of Egypt therefore, after death, was thought to become Osiris and partake of his kingdom in the hereafter. The whole body of funerary beliefs were devised originally for the king's survival after death and he alone had expectation of eternal life in the company of the great gods. As time went on however, the nobles in his entourage, and then a large number of what might be called the middle class aspired to similar privileges in the hereafter; by the New Kingdom, 'the Osiris So-and-So' became the common designation for 'the late Mr So-and-So'. But Osiris was also the judge of the dead, and in the tombs of king and commoner alike, the deceased is shown in the presence of the divine Assessors before whom he had to account for his life on earth. The virtues which he claimed to possess and the sins which he repudiated, are those which the didactic literary texts copied by schoolboys also emphasize: patience and moderation, respect for age, generosity to the poor and oppressed, fair dealing and truthful speaking, are the virtues praised. In these teachings we glimpse a code of ethics not unlike those of the modern world.

The likeable character and gay temperament of the ancient Egyptians shines through their art and their literature, and is reflected in the bright colours of the ornaments they wore and the beauty of the objects of their daily use. Much in their religion may have been gloomy, even repellent, but an incurable optimism radiates even from the tombs and a sense of humour everywhere breaks through the solemnity. Above all, they held the firm belief that the sun shone on Egypt and the Nile flowed for the benefit of its people, and that the gods would care for them:

> *Hail to thee, Ra, Lord of Truth,*
> *whose sanctuary is hidden, lord of gods...*
> *who hears the prayer of him who is in captivity,*
> *who is kindly of heart when one calls upon him,*
> *who saves the weak from the strong, the meek from the*
>   *haughty,*
> *for love of whom the Nile comes*
> *Lord of Sweetness, great in love,*
> *at whose coming the people live.*

The modern science of Egyptology may be said to have begun with the Emperor Napoleon. With his expedition to Egypt in the early years of the nineteenth century came an army of French savants whose task was to record and to investigate the country's natural history and antiquities. The results of their researches were published in thirty six weighty volumes, and gave impetus to the exploration and study of Egypt's past. In the western Delta, at Rosetta, some soldiers discovered a very precious document: a decree, inscribed on a slab of black basalt, in Greek and also in two ancient Egyptian scripts, the hieroglyphic and the cursive demotic. This trilingual text provided scholars in several countries with their first clue to the decipherment of the Egyptian script and language. Among them were the Englishman, Thomas Young, and the Frenchman Jean-François Champollion whose knowledge of Coptic (the form of the ancient language still surviving in the liturgy of the Christian church in Egypt) helped him to elucidate several royal names mentioned in the decree and to deduce therefrom the principles on which the hieroglyphic system of writing was constructed. Champollion died in 1832 at the early age of 42, after only ten years of work on his great discovery, but others carried on his work and by the middle of the nineteenth century it was already possible to decipher and understand correctly many of the ancient texts and to compile grammars and vocabularies, and to write an outline history. Meanwhile antiquaries ransacked the ancient sites; much was discovered but in the absence of scientific methods of excavation much was lost, for the careless or ignorant investigator can destroy evidence in the course of his search.

In the year 1850 another young Frenchman, by the name of Auguste Mariette, was sent out to Egypt to buy Coptic manuscripts for the Louvre in Paris. Finding archaeology more to his taste than haggling for texts, he started to dig in the area of the great cemeteries at Saqqara, near the site of Memphis, once the capital of ancient Egypt. Traces of an avenue of sphinxes reminded him of a passage from the Greek writer Strabo 'There is also a Serapeum at Memphis in a place so sandy that the winds pile up the sands, beneath which we saw the sphinxes buried up to their heads.' Here then, argued Mariette, might be found the famous necropolis of the sacred Apis bulls, successive incarnations of a god whose popularity in Graeco-Roman times had brought pilgrims from far and near. Success rewarded his enthusiasm. He found the entrance, flanked with a semicircle of statues, and some months later penetrated into the vaults where the sacred bulls had been interred in huge granite sarcophagi.

The news of his discovery made newspaper headlines and he was permitted to continue his excavations. In 1858 he was given official status by the Khedive, as Conservator of Monuments, and his life was thenceforth dedicated to the excavation and preservation of the antiquities of Egypt. His successor, Gaston Maspero, carried on his work; to him was largely due the building of a Museum of Egyptian Antiquities worthy to house the huge number of works of art now enriching the national collections, and furnished with laboratories and workshops for their treatment and preservation. The science of Egyptology achieved popularity in Europe and America; learned societies were formed and expeditions sent out. Perhaps the most spectacular of all archaeological discoveries was that of the unplundered tomb of King Tutankhamun, found by Howard Carter after years of patient search. The importance of this find for the history of Egyptian art was immeasurable and its impact on the public was immediate; excitement grew as one treasure after another was brought to light. But it added little to the sum of knowledge of Egypt's history. The story had already been pieced together, bit by bit, through the painstaking work of philologists working on the texts and of archaeologists studying the material remains.

The soil of Egypt is not yet exhausted; it has more treasures to be unearthed. As recently as the years 1968-70 the late Professor W B Emery, excavating at Saqqara for the Egypt Exploration Society and the Egyptian Antiquities Service, discovered a labyrinth of galleries in one of which the sacred cows, the mothers of Mariette's Apis bulls, had been buried. The last chapter in the history of the civilization of Ancient Egypt has not yet been written.

Brief note: – Old Kingdom (2664-2155 BC) covered Dynasties III–VIII.

Middle Kingdom (2052-1786 BC) covered Dynasty XII.

New Kingdom (1554-1075 BC) covered Dynasties XVIII–XX.

*Margaret Drower*

# I
# CREATOR GODS, AND THE CENTRES OF RELIGIOUS THOUGHT

1

*Plate 1*

The two gods of the Nile shown here were really one god, Hapi, one of the few who was common to all Egypt and part of no theological system. He was invoked to ensure the annual flooding of the great river which made the fields fertile and fed the people. Hapi was represented with the body of a man, vigorous but fleshy, and with a woman's breasts, combining in one image both aspects of fertility. The god on the left wears a crown of lotus plants; he represents the Nile in Upper Egypt. The one on the right, wearing a crown of papyrus, the Nile in Lower Egypt. The carving is a symbolic picture of the union of the two parts of Egypt – the two Hapis are binding the ties of lotus and papyrus. The carving comes from the pedestal beneath the huge statues of Rameses II in front of the great temple at Abu Simbel. Nineteenth Dynasty.

2

*Plate 2*

One of the most important documents to have
survived from the beginnings of Egyptian history
is the slate palette of King Narmer. The reverse,
shown here, depicts the king brandishing a mace
over a fallen captive – a victory motive that
occurs again and again in Egyptian art. Narmer was
a king of Upper Egypt who subdued Lower
Egypt and the Nile delta; the crown he wears
would later be combined with that of the defeated
people and produce the more familiar diadem which
the god Atum can be seen wearing in the next
picture. Particularly interesting here is the falcon
in the top right corner, leading a captive by the
nose and trampling on delta plants to signify
the subjugation of the region. The falcon is Horus,
and every succeeding pharaoh claimed to be his
earthly embodiment. The palette comes from
Hierakonpolis and is now in the Cairo Museum.
First Dynasty.

*Plate 3*

3

The three great pyramids seen through a dawn
haze. More than any other feature they epitomize
ancient Egypt in the minds of Europeans, and it was
probably no mere caprice on the part of the
pharaohs who built these tremendous tombs that
they should have taken their singular shape.
The religion of ancient Egypt was a synthesis,
developed over centuries, of the main elements of
total religions which arose in four different cities:
Heliopolis, Memphis, Hermopolis and Thebes.
A feature common to all of them was the belief
that life began on the primeval hill that rose out of
Nun – the primeval waters. The pyramids were
probably symbolic representations of the primeval
mound. The great pyramids are at Giza: the one
in the foreground is that of Mykerinus with, in
front, the small pyramids of three of his queens;
next is the pyramid of Khephren – which looks the
largest because it stands on higher ground than the
one behind it; the third is the greatest of all, that of
Kheops. The three pharaohs were of the Fourth
Dynasty.

4

*Plate 4*

Atum, the god of Heliopolis. His coming was interpreted in various ways: he formed himself out of his own will; he arose from the primeval waters; he came, and found nowhere to stand, so he created a hill (the primeval mound); he came out of the darkness, bringing light to the world. Since one of his names was Ra-Atum he was necessarily connected with the sun which was so important in the religion of ancient Egypt. He created more gods by mating with himself – the *Pyramid Texts* of the fifth century BC suggest that he was regarded as bisexual or, so to speak, both-sexual; the Egyptians saw the process of creation in sexual terms so the first god would logically be of both sexes. Atum here wears the *pschent* – the double crown of the pharaohs, and embraces the Twelfth Dynasty pharaoh Sesostris I. The Egyptian kings were fond of having themselves portrayed as the object of the gods' affections. Sesostris is on the left.

*Plate 5*

Shu, son of Atum and god of the air, who was born when his father spat him out. He can be seen in this portion of the papyrus of Pa-Shebut-n-Mut, who was a musician priestess of Amon-Ra in the Twenty-First Dynasty. The papyrus depicts the funeral rites of the priestess; the tiny figure on the extreme left is in fact a representation of her soul. Shu holds aloft the emblem of the sun-disk, and protects the soul on its voyage across the desert plateau, represented by the wavy lines of sand. On the right are the rudders of heaven and the eye of Ra. Atum also brought forth a daughter, Tefnut, sometimes described as a rain goddess but in the myths fulfilling the all-important place of a consort for Shu her brother. The papyrus is in the British Museum.

*Plate 6*

The rising sun supported by the air. At dawn the sun was likened to a scarab beetle rolling the sun before him just as a scarab beetle rolls a ball of dung. In this manifestation he was Khepri, seen here in the solar barque supported on the arms of Shu, while the sun itself is received by the sky-goddess Nut. The Egyptians believed that the ball pushed by the scarab beetle contained an egg, therefore the beetle was renewed of its own substance. So the scarab became identified with Atum the creator. The illustration is from a copy of the ancient Egyptian *Book of the Dead*, now in the British Museum.

5

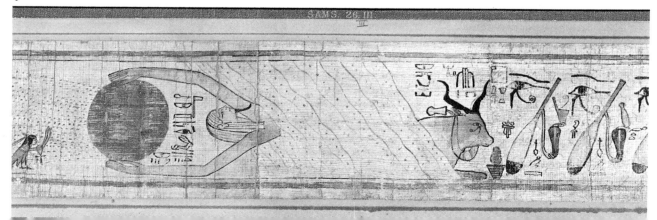

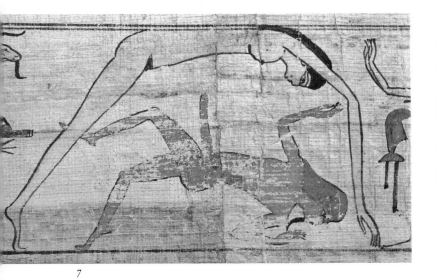

7

*Plate 7*

Shu and Tefnut became the parents of Geb, the earth, and his sister Nut, the sky. Another tradition has it that they were the children of Ra, the sun at full strength. Before the present world was made Geb and Nut were coupling and this for some reason aroused the wrath of Ra; he ordered Shu (as the god of air) to separate them, and with a great wind Shu complied. Nut was lifted off her recumbent lover and her body formed the arch of the sky. Geb, lying propped up on one elbow and with bent knee, formed the earth with its mountains and valleys. In this papyrus painting of the Twenty-first Dynasty he is seen to be green, the usual colour given to him as a vegetation god. The papyrus is in the British Museum.

*Plate 8*

As power shifted from city to city in the long course of Egyptian history the deities of the ascendant city assumed the leading place. Heliopolis was to give way to Memphis, and in time the centre of power was vested in Thebes, the city of the greatest pharaohs and the god Amon. Rameses II ruled from Thebes and he also built the great temples at Abu Simbel, where the tomb of his queen, Nefertari, was decorated with superb pictures of the gods. It can be seen that the older ones, like Atum, were never forgotten; the major figure here is Osiris since the painting is in a tomb – but the god on the right wearing the double crown is Atum. In his right hand he carries the *ankh*, the symbol of life. Nineteenth Dynasty.

8
9

*Plate 9*

The lion-headed Sekhmet receives offerings of lotus flowers from Imen-m-hebra and members of his family. This relief carving from a family tomb is now in the Cairo Museum and is notable for two reasons: it shows Sekhmet as the chosen deity of a family – not the role, the myths suggest, that she was most suitable for; and the offering of lotus flowers personifies her son Nefertum who completes the Memphis triad of gods (Ptah was his father). Sekhmet was the defender of the divine order, and she was sent forth as a lioness to chastise mankind on the occasion when they neglected to honour the gods. Unfortunately she set about the task with such relish that the supreme god had to intervene lest she destroy mankind completely.

10

*Plate 10*

A wall painting from the tomb of Sennofer
at Thebes. Sennofer was the keeper of the royal
gardens during the reign of Thuthmosis III, and
he is seen here with his sister, Merit, at his side.
He holds to his nostrils the lotus, the symbol of
rebirth and the personification of Nefertum whose
name means 'lotus'. Nefertum was a god of
Hermopolis, an ancient city to the south of Memphis
which gave many gods in their first form to
Egypt. He was adopted by the Memphis priests
to complete the triad and to stress his father
Ptah's role as the creator – it was apt that the
creator's son should symbolize rebirth. Eighteenth
Dynasty.

*Plate 11*

When King Narmer subdued Lower Egypt
he built a new capital for the united country.
The site he chose was at the apex of the Nile
Delta and the new city was called Memphis.
The high god of this region was Ptah, master
of destiny and creator of the world. The gods
of Heliopolis were, as far as the new city
was concerned, merely manifestations of him.
In this representation, a bronze statue now in the
British Museum, Ptah can be seen in his most
familiar form – that is with his legs and arms close
to his body. This is believed to be an indication of
his antiquity; his likeness was first fashioned before
men knew how to model arms and legs as
separate limbs. Memphis was a great trading centre
and the city's chief god, the patron of stonemasons,
metalworkers, boatbuilders, etc. was also the
Divine Artificer. Ptah was the rare example of an
Egyptian god who created by spiritual means
rather than physical; and while he never ceased to
command respect he was never a favourite with
ordinary people. He is seen carrying a composite
sceptre uniting the emblems of life, stability
and power.

11

12

*Plate 12*

The creation myths of Hermopolis, like those
of Heliopolis and Memphis, speak of a primeval
mound. At Hermopolis the main temple site
stood near a sacred lake and in the lake was a
small island – the primeval mound and a great place
for pilgrimages. To this mound, in the time of
chaos, came the celestial goose, the 'Great
Cackler' who broke the silence of the universe.
He laid an egg and from this was born Ra, sun god
and creator of the world. (The shell from which
he emerged was preserved at Hermopolis and
shown to pilgrims). The Great Cackler was also
the emblem of Geb, the Heliopolitan god of the
earth, and can be seen in plate 7. The ancient
traditions of Egypt were transferred happily from
centre to centre; Amon of Thebes was also
associated with the goose. The geese shown here
are from a very ancient tomb at Maidum, and
are now in the Cairo Museum. Third Dynasty,
2,600-2,500 BC.

13

*Plate 13 and 14*

Another bird which was said to have laid the cosmic egg was the ibis. This was a belief that held sway in Hermopolis and the god the ibis represented was Thoth. But a civilization which produced such a proliferation of beliefs inevitably produced a proliferation of traditions too – Thoth was also a god of Heliopolis; and another tradition, which said that Thoth was self-begotten and appeared at the beginning of time in a lotus flower, is attributed to the Hermopolitans. A god of wisdom, god of the moon, inventor of speech, patron god of scribes, the Divine Recorder – so many functions were attributed to him that it is evident that Thoth was a synthesization of a number of gods from various parts of Egypt who in their own region fulfilled these functions. One that is definitely identifiable is the ancient moon god Asten who was shown in the form of a baboon, a form in which Thoth was frequently depicted. His ibis form is shown in the bronze statue, his baboon form in a tomb painting from Tuna Gebel.

14

15

*Plate 15*

Lotus columns from the great temple at Thebes (present-day Karnak). The great god of Hermopolis was Ra, and the myth relates that a lotus rose from the primeval waters. The lotus flowered, and when its petals opened a child was disclosed, borne on the calix, who was Ra. Another version of his birth says that the flower opened and revealed a scarab beetle, the symbol of the sun. The beetle turned into a boy, who wept, and his tears were mankind. The sun symbolism, already noted in the story of Khepri, is explicit here: the lotus is a flower which opens in the sun and closes when the sun sets. Nineteenth Dynasty.

*Plate 16 and 17*

About 1,600 BC the centre of power in ancient
Egypt shifted to Thebes, the site of which is now
spread over the present-day Luxor and Karnak.
Here also, as in the centres already described, there
was a firm belief that everything began on the
primeval mound: the city of Thebes stood on it,
according to the priests. The ascendancy of Thebes
occurred when recorded history in Egypt was
already 2,000 years old and this enormous span of
time had made it possible for the high gods of
Heliopolis, Memphis and Hermopolis to be totally
accepted by the people at large. The priests of
the new capital, determined that its religious order
should lead as effectively as the political,
insisted that all other gods derived from the great
god of Thebes, Amon, who until then had no more
than local importance. Amon's first appearance in
the world was in the head and skin of a ram – the
creature which in that region had most importance
as a symbol of fertility. The illustration shows the
avenue of ram-headed sphinxes which led to the
great temple of Amon at Thebes, and some of the
tremendous columns of the hypostyle hall.
These were twelve feet in diameter and nearly
seventy feet in height; each one was elaborately
carved. The hall was 330 feet long and 170 feet
deep – but this enormous structure, an achievement
to be compared with the building of the pyramids,
is only one example of the grandeur of the
Theban period. Each pharaoh, anxious for
immortality, made a contribution of his own and
sometimes enlarged and embellished the temples
of his predecessors. Nineteenth Dynasty.

16

17

18

*Plate 18*

The goddess Neith, wearing the crown of Lower Egypt. Like the ram-headed Khnum and the Nile god Hapi she was a 'separate' deity; she was probably the original Earth Mother of the Delta region. During the long centuries of Egyptian religious history she is encountered again and again, usually as an addition, or as a useful auxiliary to one of the prevailing systems. One tradition makes her the mother of Isis, Osiris and Horus; another gives her a place in the Osiris cult as one of the attendant deities in the funeral rites. She makes a notable appearance in the story of Horus and Set when, as the source of ancient wisdom, her counsel is sought. Her cult enjoyed a notable revival in the Twenty-sixth Dynasty, when the pharaoh Nectanebo II proclaimed himself the son of Neith, and royal burials took place at Sais in the Delta. The eyes of this statue, of the Twenty-fifth Dynasty, are inlaid with silver.

*Plate 19*

The Step Pyramid at Saqqara which was built by Imhotep to house the tomb of his master, the Third Dynasty pharaoh Djoser. During the reign of Djoser there was a famine which lasted for seven years; Imhotep, his vizier, advised him to go to Elephantine where the Nile waters were divided by Khnum, half going to the south and half to the north. Djoser was visited by Khnum in a dream, and told that the God's sanctuaries were neglected. The pharaoh thereupon donated all the land on either side of Elephantine and all the produce of the area to the further glory of Khnum. He also built a magnificent temple on the island itself. The Nile waters rose again, for the first time in seven years, and the famine came to an end.

*Plate 20*

Khnum, one of the several ram-headed gods of Egyptian mythology. The strange curling horns with their horizontal projection belonged to a species which is no longer extant, and the recurrence of this image in Egyptian iconography suggests that the ram-headed gods – with the exception of Amon – date back to the beginning of recorded history. Khnum was an ancient god of the First Cataract of the Nile where, on the island of Elephantine, the river was said to emerge from the subterranean ocean of Nun. Self-created, Khnum was in some traditions the maker of earth, water and the underworld. He created both god and men; he fashioned men from clay on a potter's wheel and every child born is formed by his hands.
Bronze statuette, now in the British Museum.

19

# II
# THE PRINCIPAL GODS

21

*Plate 21*

Ra, the sun god of Heliopolis, seen in an inlaid bronze aegis of the Ptolemaic period. Called the Father of the Gods, Ra once ruled on earth during a golden age when men and gods could live together happily. While he was in his full vigour the order of the universe seemed immutable but there came a time when even he, the supreme god, had to yield to another – the events recounted in the story of Horus and Set. Each morning Ra, as the sun, rose in the east and set off across the world, to sink below the horizon in the west. He was often shown as a disk, borne on a boat – the solar barque – but the most familiar representation was perhaps as a man with a falcon's head or as a falcon.

*Plate 22*

The adoration of Ra, from The *Book of the Dead* of Hunefer, now in the British Museum. The sun god appears over the eastern horizon and is received by seven figures of Thoth, in his form as a baboon. He carries on his head the solar disk with the uraeus symbol – the emblem of all the the pharaohs' power. In the lower half of the picture is the djed-column which represents Osiris; on the left is Isis and on the right is Nephthys. Early Nineteenth Dynasty.

*Plate 23*

A leaf from the papyrus of Ani, an Eighteenth Dynasty *Book of the Dead* in the British Museum. At the top of the leaf are two pictures of Ra proceeding on his journey. On the right the solar barque travels as the bright sun of day; the picture on the left shows the approach of night – the strength of the sun diminishes and the stars appear as the sky grows dark. Eventually the barque entered the realm of night and met the powers of darkness. The chief of these was the serpent Apep who tried to swallow the barque; a nightly struggle ensued, and when the sun reappeared on the eastern horizon the next day prayers of thankfulness were offered that Ra was triumphant and the sun would continue to shine. The sun god was often called Ra-Harakhte, or Horus of the Horizon: Horus was an early sun god always depicted as a falcon.

22
23

*Plate 24*

The sun god is frequently seen in copies of the *Book of the Dead* and in wall paintings from tombs and mortuary temples. This may seem odd since modern thinking does not normally connect a sun god with death. His presence in so many of them is explained by the tradition that Ra always sent his son Anubis to prepare the body of Osiris for burial, and by the fact that the sun sank over the western horizon at night – Ra-Harakhte showed the way to the world of the dead. This illustration is from the tomb of Nefertari, the queen of Rameses II, at Abu Simbel. On the left is the goddess Hathor, Ra's daughter, wearing on her head the sign of a falcon on a perch which meant the west where the dead were buried. On the right is Ra-Harakhte wearing the sun disk and uraeus, and holding the *ankh* in his right hand. Nineteenth Dynasty.

*Plate 25 and 26*

The goddess Hathor. An ancient sky goddess, she was first represented as a cow; later she was shown as a woman with a cow's head, and then simply as a goddess as in the preceding picture. In the myths she and Isis are often confused: Hathor in some traditions is the mother of Horus, though the stronger and more important myth of Isis and Osiris gives the mother's part to Isis. But confusion is further increased by the habit of some iconographers of portraying Isis with cow's horns. However the cow attribute is principally Hathor's and she was often described as the *nurse* of Horus, which led to the pictures of her as a cow suckling the pharaoh. The one thus engaged is Amenhotep II, in a wall painting from his tomb. Hathor was also believed to suckle the dead, to sustain them on their journey to the next world, a function depicted in the mural from the tomb of Rameses VI in the Valley of the Kings. Hathor was the goddess of light-hearted pleasure and love, and of music and dancing.

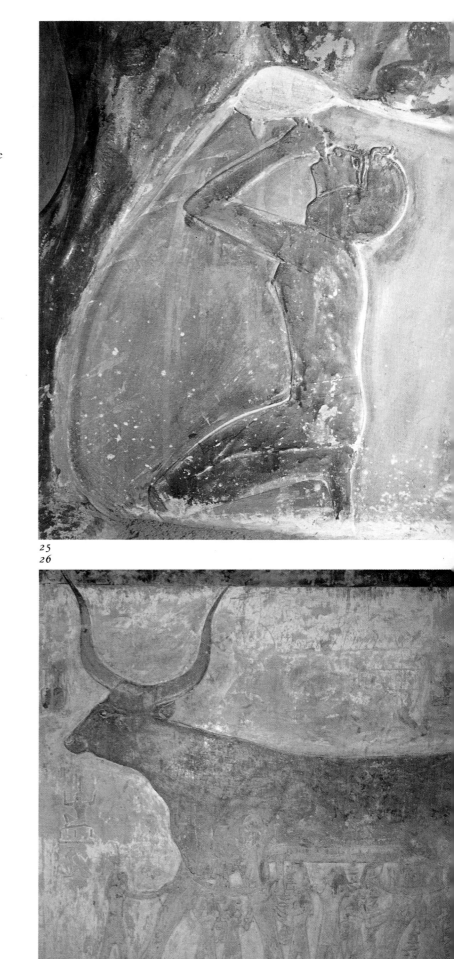

25
26

27

*Plate 27*

Detail of a colossal statue of Rameses II at Karnak, showing the pharaoh as the god Osiris. (The pharaohs had no modesty whatever about such matters, as the pictures in this book will testify. In any case they believed themselves to be the 'living' Horus; a great deal would follow from that).

Osiris was an ancient fertility god with a very widespread cult. The myths surrounding him say that he was the son of Nut and Geb, and at his birth the all-powerful Ra acknowledged him as his heir. He brought civilization to Egypt and taught the people how to cultivate the food plants. He was married to Isis, his sister, and she ruled the country with equal success whenever Osiris was absent spreading his civilizing mission to other peoples. The god Set was brother to Osiris; Nephthys was his sister. Nineteenth Dynasty.

28

*Plate 28*

The goddess Isis holding a sistrum. This painted relief is from a temple built at Abydos by the pharaoh Seti I, the father of Rameses II. Isis was most venerated as the wife of Osiris and the mother of Horus but she had an equal reputation as the Enchantress. Her magic was allied to the wisdom of Thoth and given to mankind as a skill in healing; she was also responsible, as the counterpart of Osiris, for teaching the household arts to women. She taught them weaving and spinning, and how to grind the corn. Her strongest appeal was as the sorrowing wife and devoted mother – every woman could identify with her and she has been seen by some commentators as the archetype of a cult that continues in the Christian churches to the present day.

*Plate 29*

A detail from a bronze statuette in the British Museum depicting Set, the brother of Osiris and the agent of his destruction. Set was one of the oldest gods of Egypt and, remarkably, retained his position as a deity while the myths credited him with every evil deed. He was jealous of the eminence of Osiris, and when the latter returned to to Egypt invited him to a banquet under the guise of friendship. Set imprisoned his brother in a chest lined with lead, and had the chest thrown into the Nile.

*Plate 30*

The chest was carried down to the sea and cast ashore on the coast of Byblos, where it lodged in the branches of a sapling. The sapling, growing into a tree, enfolded the chest, and eventually the tree was cut down and made into a beautiful column for the king's palace. Isis was able to divine where the chest was and she made her way to Byblos; she used her skills and her magic crafts to secure a place at court and was made nurse of the royal child. At night she became a swallow, flying round the beautiful column and mourning Osiris. (The picture is a detail from the painted coffin of Seni, *c* 2,000 BC, now in the British Museum). Isis also tried to give the royal child immortality by burning his mortal attributes; but the queen came upon her and screamed in terror which prevented the process from being completed. Isis revealed herself; she was given the chest from the column and allowed to go back to Egypt.

29

30

31

Plate 31

Isis hid the chest in the marshes of the Delta but it was discoverd by Set when he was out hunting. He smashed the chest and cut the body to pieces, distributing them over a vast area; his hope was that they could never be assembled and his revenge would be complete. But Isis called on Set's wife, the goddess Nephthys, to help her – Nephthys was sister to both Isis and Osiris. The two roamed over the land and painfully collected the pieces, reassembling them to make the first mummy.

This part of the Osiris myth became an integral part of Egyptian burial rites, and can be seen in this painting from the tomb of Sennutem, a member of the royal household during the Nineteenth Dynasty. Protecting the dead man are those who mourned for Osiris – Isis and Nephthys, in the form of kites.

32

*Plate 32*

Despite her great powers, Isis was unable to bring Osiris back to life. Yet her gifts were formidable enough to enable her to concieve a child by him, and in due time Horus was born. Set discovered this and soon Isis was aware that she was watched constantly by her enemy, who intended to kill the child when the opportunity came. Isis, determined that her son should live to take his father's place, invoked the protection of Ra, who sent down Thoth from the solar barque. The sun halted in the heavens and Isis was promised that all would be well. Osiris remained a king – in the other world, and all men in dying hoped that they would aspire to his honoured company. Osiris is seen here as the divine mummy, wearing the *atef* crown. He carries the crook and flail, symbols of royalty, and on either side are two funeral sacrifices and two columns. The Eyes of Ra look down on him and the lotus symbol of rebirth stands before him. Painting from the tomb of Sennutem. Nineteenth Dynasty.

33

*Plate 33*

Isis and Osiris. The divine couple portrayed on a painted relief in the mortuary temple of the pharaoh Seti I at Abydos. Osiris is seated and Isis stands behind his chair. The pharaoh is behind Isis, with his back to her, and overhead, in full flight, is the vulture goddess Nekhebet. A protective goddess of Upper Egypt, Nekhebet's function were particularly associated with the monarchs; she can be seen here holding the royal ring in her talons. The relief is from the Horus shrine of the temple, which is of the Nineteenth Dynasty.

*Plate 34*

Isis and Horus. Isis, wearing cow horns and the sun disk, is suckling the infant Horus, who is oddly represented as an adult pharaoh. Statues of Isis were generally portraits of the reigning queen, which is why the goddess is shown wearing the *uraeus*. The infant Horus was sometimes portrayed as a child wearing the pharaonic crown and with a finger to his lips. This group is bronze, of the Nineteenth Dynasty, and is now in the Abbey Museum, New Barnet.

35

36

*Plate 35*

Isis, from the shrine of Tutankhamun. There was a tradition that she protected the dead Osiris with long feathery wings that, as the Great Enchantress, she was able to grow. Another says that it was with her wings that she attempted to transmit to him the breath of life. Inevitably, she was adopted as one of the protector goddesses in funeral rites and frequently depicted with her sister Nephthys, similarly winged, their plumaged arms entwined. Carved wood, overlaid with gold. Eighteenth Dynasty.

*Plate 36*

Like all the principal gods of Egypt – with the possible exception of Osiris – Horus had many forms. The god of ancient times seen on the palette of King Narmer brought the falcon's head, and the association with Ra the sun disk; but in addition to those forms there were local deities absorbed by him, and old gods who in some form represented the sun. One of these was Haroeris, or Horus the Elder, variously the son or husband of Hathor, and easily confused with the son of Isis and Osiris. Originally Haroeris was a god of light, whose eyes were the sun and moon. Sometimes there was no moon, of course, and Haroeris became the patron god of the blind. Bronze statuette of the Twenty-sixth Dynasty, now in the British Museum.

*Plate 37*

As Harmahkis, Horus personified the rising sun. The name means Horus on the Horizon. He is seen here in the most famous sculpture in the world, the great Sphinx at Giza which was carved out of the solid rock near the pyramid of Khephren. The height of the Sphinx is sixty-five feet, and is believed to be a portrait of Khephren himself. Harmakhis was believed to be not only the sun god rising but also the repository of great wisdom, and a symbol of resurrection. The pharaoh Tuthmosis IV, as a young prince, fell asleep in the shadow of the Sphinx, and dreamed that Harmakhis entreated him to clear away the sand that was building up and threatening to engulf him; the god would award him the throne of Egypt in return. A stele was later uncovered on the site which bore out the details of the story. Tuthmosis declared that he owed his throne to Harmakhis, and this was to have dramatic consequences for the succeeding pharaohs of the Eighteenth Dynasty. (see plate 64.) The Sphinx was carved during the Fourth Dynasty.

37

38

Plate 38

Horus as a falcon. The great sky god's statue
stands in the court of his temple at Edfu in Upper
Egypt. His close connection with the pharaohs is
stressed by his headdress, the double crown of
Egypt. As a child, Horus narrowly escaped being
destroyed by Set, who had murdered his father
Osiris. As a man, he claimed his father's rank and,
further, the leadership of the gods when Ra
(as Ra-Harakhte) grew old. Set contested this
claim, and demanded that Horus should justify it in
combat. Ra wanted Set, as the god with the most
authority, to be his successor; but most of the gods
favoured Horus. When some of them, with scant
respect, pointed out to Ra that his shrines were
empty he retired from the debate in a bad temper.

39

40

*Plate 39*

Nothing would induce Ra to rejoin the discussion and the whole matter was halted. It was the goddess Hathor who coaxed him out of his sulks; she went to his arbour and performed a striptease. This cheered him up and he returned to the meeting, where he demanded that Set and Horus should put their cases in an orderly way for due consideration. The case for Set was strong, many agreeing with him that the throne of Osiris was too great a challenge for one as young as Horus. The illustration is from the tomb of Rameses VI. The goddess Hathor is seen holding the sun in one hand and man in the other. Twentieth Dynasty.

*Plate 40*

Eventually the struggle was joined and Set, older in cunning than Horus, came very close to being the victor. But he lacked an ally to equal the one Horus could call upon – the great Isis who was determined that her son should inherit the throne of Osiris. She guided him through every phase of the struggle, and turned the tables on Set when, under the pretence of peace-making, he attempted to rape Horus, knowing that this would discredit him in the eyes of the other gods. Isis knew that Set had a great liking for lettuce, so she prepared a dish of crisp green leaves. Set ate the dish with pleasure – and conceived, to the great mirth of the company when it became known. Isis had added the seed of Horus to the lettuce leaves.
The great goddess is seen here in a painted relief from the tomb of Amun-kher-khopsh, one of the sons of Rameses III. She embraces Rameses, who wears the blue *khepresh* or war helmet of the pharaohs. Twentieth Dynasty.

41

*Plate 41*

In spite of his mother's help Horus never managed
to defeat Set decisively, and in the end the gods
decided to appeal to Osiris himself. Osiris rebuked
the gods: he said that his son was the rightful heir,
and that the very food eaten by man and gods
depended on the good offices of Osiris. Ra scoffed
at that, declaring that the food plants and food
animals would have been on the earth if Osiris
had never existed. Osiris returned that his authority
could not be challenged; that everyone would
eventually rest with Osiris when they passed to the
West, the land of the dead where he was judge.
This decided the issue and Horus thus inherited his
father's place. He re-established the reign of Mayet
– justice – which Osiris declared had been cast down.
Set was given the charge of the wind and storms.
Horus is seen with his father Osiris in this relief
from a temple at Abydos of the Nineteenth
Dynasty.

*Plate 42*

One of the gods who favoured the case of Horus
was Anhur, a local deity from the country near
Abydos who became associated with the Osiris
cult. Variously the creative power of the sun and the
warlike aspect of Ra, he was identified by the
Greeks with Ares. Probably his right arm, upraised,
originally carried a lance; some representations gave
him a cord by which he led the sun. A popular
god with ordinary people, Anhur was the
'Saviour' and the 'Good Warrior' who gave
protection against enemies, both human and animal.
As a war god, his cult became powerful in the New
Empire (Eighteenth to Twenty-fourth Dynasties)
and flourished for nearly sixteen centuries – right up
to the end of the Ptolemaic period when Egypt
came under the domination of Rome. Statuette of
the Twenty-fifth Dynasty, now in the British
Museum.

42

43

*Plate 43*

Thoth. The ibis-headed god seen in a painted relief from the temple of Amon at Karnak, pouring the water of life from a vase. In addition to his function as a moon god and the inventor of speech Thoth was credited with considerable magic powers, and these were called upon by Isis herself in the story of Horus and Set. He also invented writing, which gave him enormous power since all wisdom came to be placed in that which was written down, and the calendar – he was the divine regulative force. The divine scribe, he was present at all funeral rites, where his function was to record the deeds of the dead man before they were placed in the scales with the feather of truth. Thoth was identified with Hermes by the Greeks. Nineteenth Dynasty.

44
45

*Plate 44*

Anubis as a black jackal with a bushy tail; a striking representation from the tomb of Tutankhamun. It is carved from wood and varnished black, with gilded decorations and eyes of alabaster and obsidian. The origin of this god probably lay in the fact that jackals could always be heard howling in the desert to the west of the Nile at sunset. The west was where the sun sank each day, and where burials usually took place. The jackal was a despoiler, as well as being associated with death, so he was propitiated, and came to be regarded as the messenger from the other world. It wasn't long before he became a god and he was always associated with death; he supervized and performed the funeral rites of Osiris which fixed the form of such ceremonies in Egyptian religion. Eighteenth Dynasty.

*Plate 45*

Buto, the cobra goddess. She is perhaps more familiarly depicted as the *uraeus* cobra worn in the pharaoh's crown, ready to deal death to his enemies. Her cult originated in the Delta and she was primarily a goddess of Lower Egypt just as the vulture goddess, Nekhebet, the other creature worn on the crown, was of Upper Egypt. Both goddesses were closely associated with the Nile. Buto was often to be seen on representations of Ra, and then she personified the sun's burning heat; she wears the sun disk in this painting from the tomb of the prince Amun-kher-khopsh in the Valley of the Kings. Twentieth Dynasty.

*Plate 46*

With their predilection for making gods of every animal they encountered the Egyptians naturally deified the crocodile, a creature familiar to people whose lives were spent by a great river and its Delta. The god was Sebek, a water god who was said to be the son of Neith. He became widely worshipped throughout Egypt after his rise to prominence in the Twelfth Dynasty (2,000 to 1,790 BC), when the pharaohs favoured the lakes and marshes of Lower Egypt. Another traditon that favoured him was that he was the form which Horus assumed when he searched for pieces of his father Osiris' body in the waters of the Nile. As a state god in the Twelfth Dynasty he became identified with the sun, and when Ra was identified with Amon after the rise of Thebes representations of Sebek began to appear with him wearing Amon's insignia – the ram's horns and the plumed headdress. Bronze of the Twenty-second Dynasty, now in the British Museum.

46

*Plate 47*

The ram was, according to the evidence of archaeology, one of the sacred beasts of the prehistoric people of the upper Nile. The creature occurs frequently in the iconography of Egypt but only Amon's representative bears a ram's form we can all recognize – an indication of his late ascendancy. Amon himself was said to have remained hidden until the times were ready for him; that is until the princes of Thebes, where he was a local deity, were ready to assume the hegemony of Egypt and make their city the capital. Their god became the great god Amon and soon all powers were ascribed to him; those of Ptah, of Ra, and of course of the erstwhile creator gods. Eighteenth Dynasty.

47

48

*Plate 48*

The goddess Mut. She was a local deity of the Thebes region, like Amon, and was the divine mother. Originally a vulture goddess, she was inevitably confused with Nehkebet; when she began to be portrayed as a woman the vulture was placed in her crown. She was a convenient goddess for the Thebans to have around – it was a simple matter to make her the consort of Amon. Their marriage was celebrated annually and on those occasions Amon made oracular pronouncements through his priests. The Greeks identified Mut with Hera. Nineteenth Dynasty sculpture, now in the Cairo Museum.

49

50

*Plate 49*

Mut can also be seen in this papyrus painting, partially obscured, standing behind Khons. The moon god of Thebes, he was the third member of that city's triad of gods; his mother was Mut and his father Amon. Here he wears the double-plumed crown of Amon. The myths surrounding him say that he was actually the afterbirth of Amon; the all-powerful sun being Amon, everything that pertained to him must have been divine, so the afterbirth became the moon. But two traditions are obviously in conflict here, since he was generally accepted as Amon's son. With Thebes in the ascendant, Khons assimilated the functions of Thoth – as the divine regulator – and of Shu – as god of the heavens and the atmosphere.

*Plate 50*

Amon giving his protection to the queen-pharaoh Hatshepsut. By the time of the Eighteenth Dynasty Amon was supreme; but, as we shall see, it was during the Eighteenth Dynasty that he was nearly overthrown. However, he survived the religious revolution and became even more powerful in the Nineteenth and the greatest pharaoh of that dynasty, Rameses II, acknowledged his might unequivocally. Amon was the god of victory, king of the gods, Lord of the Thrones of the World – all his titles were a recognition of Egypt's greatness during the Eighteenth Dynasty; stretching from the Euphrates to the Sudan, it was the greatest power of the ancient world. Nevertheless, in spite of all the power and grandeur associated with his name, Amon was a popular god with the people, who saw him as the protector of the poor and the weak.

*Plate 51*

Bast, the cat goddess, was a very ancient deity; she has been identified in the antiquities of the Second Dynasty – that means that she was worshipped as long ago as 3,200 BC. Her cult was in the Delta, at the city of Bubastis, and the pharaohs of the Twenty-second Dynasty, deciding to rule from there, made her a state deity. Bubastis was enriched and a new temple to Bast was built at Thebes. Her origins may have lain in the fact that the people of the Delta – a region frequented by snakes of many kinds – welcomed the wild cat, a killer of snakes, into their homes. The cat took readily to domestication. One myth says that Bast accompanied the solar barque through the regions of night, and nightly gave battle to the serpent Apep, the enemy of Ra. There was a cemetery of mummified cats at Bubastis which was noted by Herodotus in the second book of his *Histories*. Bronze of the Twenty-second Dynasty.

52

*Plate 52*

A Twelfth Dynasty relief carving from Thebes showing Sesostris I and the god Min. A god of fertility, Min was particularly the bestower of sexual powers in men, and at Abu Simbel a number of murals feature him being offered lettuce by the pharaoh; lettuce was believed to be an aphrodisiac in ancient Egypt and it was fed regularly to the white bulls (the sacred animals of Min) during the harvest celebrations. Min was the bringer of rain, and the generative force in nature – particularly he was associated with the growth and ripening of grain. At Thebes he was often shown wearing the crown of Amon and carrying a flail in one hand.

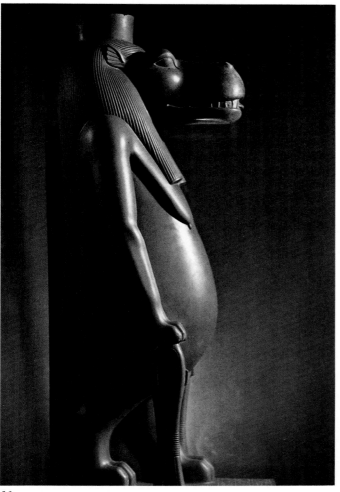

53

*Plate 53*

Taueret was a mother goddess of prehistoric times, and in spite of her grotesque association with the hippopotamus she was always revered as the protective deity of expectant mothers and of women in childbirth. Through later myths she acquired connections with the daily reappearance of Ra in the solar barque but her real strength lay in her role as a domestic goddess. Amulets of Tauret were placed in tombs to invoke her protection when the deceased was reborn in the kingdom of the dead.
Her connection with Ra was also one of rebirth – the sun reborn every day on the eastern horizon.
Here she is seen with the *sa*, the symbol of protection, in her right hand. Twenty-sixth Dynasty statuette from Thebes, now in the Cairo Museum.

*Plate 54*

Bes, the dwarf god who brought happiness to the home. He first appeared in Egypt in the Twelfth Dynasty (2,000 - 1,790 BC), and is believed to have originated in the Sudan; he is sometimes shown wearing a lion or leopard skin. The protector of the family, he was a friend to all women; he presided over their toilet, marriage, and at childbirth was on hand to drive away evil spirits. He was a merry god who danced and made music and in imitation of this his festivals were always gay occasions. He was most frequently depicted on head-boards of beds – particularly of marriage beds – and he is seen here as the terminal of an elaborately carved staff of the Twenty-first Dynasty.

*Plate 55*

Selket was originally one of the protective goddesses of the four sources of the Nile. These arose from the nether regions, and eventually Selket became one of the guardian goddesses at burials; she is seen here at one of the most famous in the world, that of the young pharaoh Tutankhamun. Her place was at the south-east side. Selket has been traced to prehistoric times and she was a goddess of fertility as well as a guardian and probably her association with the scorpion dates from then. Like the jackal, the scorpion was feared, so it was propitiated; from there to being made a deity was a short step for the Egyptians. The statue is carved from wood, and gilded. Eighteenth Dynasty.

*Plate 56*

Mayet, the goddess who personified justice and truth, who stood between illusion and reality, good and evil. When she was not honoured chaos came again.

Mayet was probably an abstraction, rather like Themis in Greek religion, but once she was named she was inevitably personified and the Egyptians regarded her as the daughter of Ra. She emerged with him from the primeval waters and replaced chaos; she was the light that Ra brought to the world. The pharaohs claimed to rule by Mayet and the ordinary people had a strong awareness of her; she was perhaps more important to them, who were ruled, than to those who ruled. Both pharaoh and commoner alike, however, knew that they would have to account to her when they died, and that their hearts would be balanced against her. (See plate 88.) Only if the scales were even would they be allowed into the presence of Osiris. The goddess is always recognized by her ostrich plume – sometimes only the plume is present in the scales in the Hall of Judgment. Mayet is also to be seen in the barque of the sun, accompanying her father Ra. Painted relief from the tomb of Seti I, Nineteenth Dynasty.

56

# III
# THE LORDS OF THE TWO LANDS

57

*Plate 57*

The rulers of Egypt, while they represented themselves as gods on earth, never attained the status in myth of their counterparts in Greece. Their lives and deeds are well documented and this, paradoxically, kept them 'earthbound' in a way that never happened to the Greeks. The pharaohs could insist on their divine particulars but, in the end, it could be seen that this was merely what they said of themselves. Nevertheless they are a part of Egypt's mythology, since one cannot encounter the gods without also meeting the all-powerful rulers who glorified them. At Saqqara, near the step pyramid of the pharaoh Dhoser, we see a frieze of cobra heads. There is a tradition that during the conflict between Horus and Set the latter succeeded in tearing out Horus' eyes; the *uraeus* symbol replaced them and became thereafter the symbol of royal power. Third Dynasty.

58

*Plate 58*

Khephren, the pharaoh who built the second pyramid, and then ordered the Sphinx to be carved from the rest of the rock. This statue, one of twenty-three which were found in the hall of the Temple of Khephren, has a lonely majesty that strongly suggests the god-king. The god Horus, as a falcon, can be seen perched behind him, transmitting his strength to his representative on earth. The statue is of green diorite. Fourth Dynasty.

59

*Plate 59*

Sesostris I is received into the embrace of the god Ptah (see the picture in plate 4, where Sesostris is embraced by the god Atum). Ptah is the figure on the left. Sesostris I favoured Heliopolis and built a great temple there but his family came from the region of Thebes and he did not neglect to honour that city. This relief came from there, part of a temple he built when he honoured the main gods of Egypt and was received into their shrines as their son. It was in his reign that a hitherto obscure god of the Theban region, Amon, began to come to the fore. The temple built by Sesostris was demolished to make way for the great temple of Amon and the relief, nearly nine feet high, became part of a heap of rubble. It is now in the Cairo Museum. Twelfth Dynasty.

60

*Plate 60*

The Valley of the Kings on the west bank of the Nile at Thebes. The pharaohs of the Eighteenth, Nineteenth and Twentieth Dynasties had their tombs there, cut out of the rock in a defile in the mountains. Some of the burial chambers were over 600 feet deep in the rock, and contained many halls and chambers; but in spite of the most elaborate complications for sealing the tombs – and curses to any who disturbed them – not a single royal burial place was ever found to be completely intact. Even the celebrated tomb of Tutankhamun, with its fabulous treasures, showed signs of having been disturbed, and it should be remembered that Tutankhamun was far from being a monarch of any significance. What the tombs of Tuthmosis III, Amenophis III, or Rameses II would have contained can only be guessed at. They were successfully plundered, with scores of others, through the centuries.

61

62

## Plate 61

The mortuary temple of Hatshepsut, the first
woman to succeed completely in reigning over
Egypt as a sovereign in her own right.
A matriarchal system of inheritance persisted in
Egypt from the earliest times, and the throne could
be gained by marriage to a royal heiress. Hatshepsut
was the daughter of Tuthmosis I, and while she
acknowledged that her brother – and husband – had
a right to the throne and saw him reign as
Tuthmosis II, she believed her own claim to follow
him to be stronger than that of her half-brother who
eventually reigned as Tuthmosis III. She had no
compunction about declaring herself the daughter of
the god Amon, and his priests must have agreed
– the people did not question their pronouncements.
This female pharaoh had elaborate reliefs carved in
the temple, picturing in detail her direct descent
from the god. Her successor took care to have the
reliefs and their accompanying inscriptions chiselled
out.

## Plate 62

Tuthmosis as pharaoh, the third of his name.
The god who was invoked by Hatshepsut to help
her gain the throne was, apparently, a fickle one.
It was with the help of the priesthood of Amon that
Tuthmosis III deposed his half-sister. Though she was
an able ruler, she earned her half-brother's undying
hatred in her scorn of him. The daughter of the first
Tuthmosis, the sister and wife of the second, she had
reason to be proud; her half-brother was merely the
child of one of her brother – husband's 'other' wives.
But the despised prince turned the tables on her with
an oracle from the priests of Amon, which
proclaimed his right to the throne. He went on to
greatness – Egypt under Tuthmosis III reached its
greatest extent and colossal wealth flowed in
from the conquered countries.

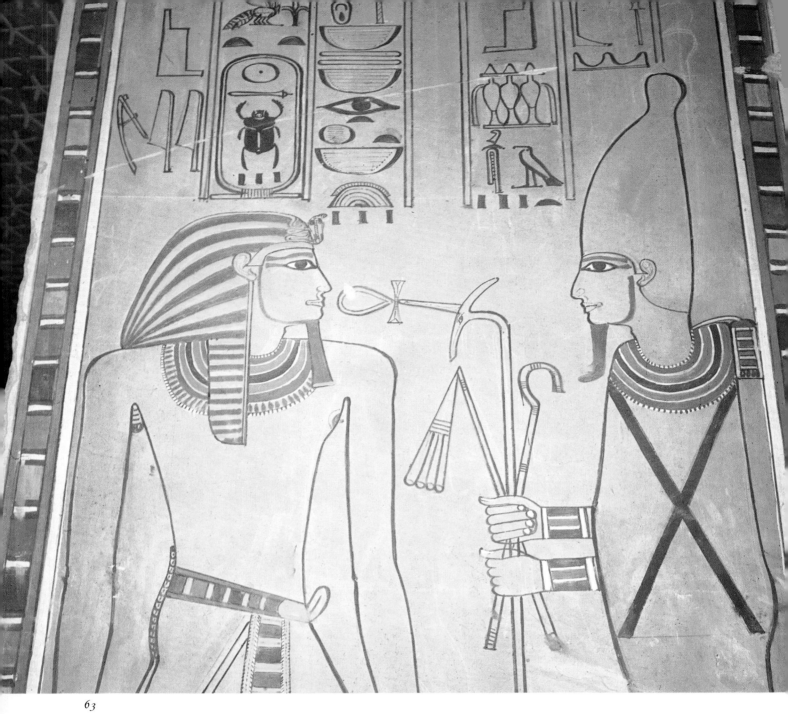

63

*Plate 63*

Toward the end of his reign Tuthmosis III tired of
the authority of Amon; that is, he tired of the priests
of Amon, and began to look to another god to
balance their power. To this end he planned a
temple in Thebes to the east of the Temple of
Amon, a temple to the rising sun. It was to contain a
single obelisk, a great needle of stone inscribed to
Ra-Harakhte, the Horus of the Horizon. This
revolutionary step – in the city of Amon – was
carefully ignored by his successor; Tuthmosis died
before the temple was completed and the obelisk lay
disregarded by the sacred lake of Thebes. The new
pharaoh, Amenophis II, is seen here in a painting
from his tomb in the Valley of the Kings. He faces
Osiris, who offers him the breath of life in the *ankh*
symbol.

*Plate 64*

At Medinet Habu, near Thebes, there can be seen the two colossal seated statues of Amenophis III. These are all that remain of the pharaoh's mortuary temple and their size – they are over sixty feet high – give some idea of what the temple could have been like in extent. The statues were carved from quartzite brought 400 miles from a quarry near Heliopolis. The reign of Amenophis III was one of splendour – Egypt was enjoying her supreme place in the ancient world; but the seed sown by Tuthmosis III had taken root and the old order was already being eroded. Despite the adherence of Amenophis II to the old ways his successor, Tuthmosis IV, had disturbed things further (see Plate 37). Harmakhis and Ra-Harakhte were aspects of the sun, and Amenophis III was sympathetic to the new beliefs. The ram-headed god was being ousted from his supreme place.

64

*Plate 65*

The revolution came with the next pharaoh, Amenophis IV. When he ascended the throne the great Eighteenth Dynasty was at its peak; when he died it was not only virtually over but sunk very low indeed. Amenophis IV pushed the idea of the sun as the supreme god farther than his predeccessors ever dreamed; the sun at its zenith, the bestower of all things was to be the *only* god. The pharaoh would naturally be his only representative – through the one god he would be immortal. The new god was *Aten* (disk), and Amenophis changed his name to Akhenaten. The statue shown here is in the Cairo Museum and represents a departure in the portrayal of the pharaohs. Ahkenaten refused to have his portraits idealized, and he was a sickly and far from comely man. Nevertheless he was shown in the Osiris position in this statue, with his arms crossed over his chest and carrying the crook and flail. It dates from the beginning of his reign, and originally stood in the temple to Ra-Harakhte which was begun by Tuthmosis III.

65

66

*Plate 66*

Akhenaten built a new city for his god lower down the Nile and called it Akhetaten. The site is close to the modern Tell el Amarna. The cult of the *aten* lasted about as long as the reign of the pharaoh who promoted it, about seventeen years. A wiser ruler might have been able to maintain his power while carrying out his religious reforms but history shows that Egypt suffered acutely in prestige during his reign. Akhenaten declared that he ruled by Mayet (the goddess personifying truth and justice) but his adherence to his personal ideals did not prevent the eroding of Egypt's frontiers or the growing unrest in Thebes, where the cult of Amon was actively persecuted. In any case, monotheism was an alien concept to the Egyptians, as we have seen. This stele from the Cairo Museum shows Akhenaten and his queen presenting offerings to Aten, who bestows the breath of life. The small figure behind the queen is one of the royal princesses, Meritaten.

67

Plate 67

Akhenaten's queen was Nefertiti, and her portrait busts show that she was a woman of remarkable beauty. The available evidence suggests that she was not an Egyptian – a striking departure for the Egyptian royal house which, to keep the line pure and to follow the example of Isis and Osiris, usually married the princes and princesses to each other. But her origins cannot be ascertained and some authorities maintain that her beauty represents to the full the ideal seen in so many of the Tombs of the Eighteenth Dynasty. Her ultimate fate is wrapped in mystery – she disappears from the visual records at some time in the last three years of the reign. This unfinished bust, itself a thing of beauty, comes from Tell el Amarna and is now in the Cairo Museum.

*Plate 68*

The death of Akhenaten was also the death of Aten as a god of any consequence. Amon resumed his supremacy in Thebes and order was restored to Egypt. Tutankhaten was given a more suitable name, and history knows him as Tutankhamun. A boy of nine, he was carefully prepared for his coronation by the priests of Amon and the officers of state, and of the gods he acknowledged as being present when he received the crown it was Amon who placed his hand on the king's neck – or so the ritual declared. The illustration shows the front panel of a painted chest from the tomb of Tutankhamun and commemorates a war against Syria during his reign.

*Plate 69*

Tutankhamun died when he was eighteen or twenty – the records are not clear – and was fated to become the most famous pharaoh in history. His life was unremarkable and his death was probably expected; neither of his predecessors was exactly robust and Tutankhamun's physical condition would have been known to his advisors. Tutankhamun is seen here in one of his funerary masks, a priceless object of beaten gold decorated with faience. He wears the *nemset* headdress and on his brow the protective goddesses Nekhebet of Upper Egypt and Buto of Lower Egypt. The treasures of his tomb, discovered in 1922, were what made the boy pharaoh famous; he himself could have been described, until then, as the most obscure of all the monarchs of Egypt.

68

*Plate 70*

The goddess Isis watches eternally. Her place was at the north-west, and three more of these exquisite gilded images were found in Tutankhamun's tomb. Selket, the scorpion goddess, had her place at the south-east, Nephthys at the south-west, and Neith at the north-east.

70

*Plate 71*

After Tutankhamun the Eighteenth Dynasty was virtually over, he was in fact the last of the legitimate line. The great god of Thebes, however, seemed eternal; Amon was as strong as he had ever been. Two pharaohs followed Tutankhamun in the Eighteenth Dynasty; Ay, who had been the vizier of Amenophis III, and Horemheb, a resolute soldier who gave Egypt a period of internal stability and peace. When he died one of his generals, Rameses, stepped into the vacant place and the Nineteenth Dynasty began. In this period Egypt recovered some of her former glory, particularly under Seti I. His successor was Rameses II, who left a display of stupendous glory that concealed for a time the fact that Egypt was truly in decline. The illustration shows a cartouche from the temple of Amon at Karnak, bearing the name, in heiroglyphics, of Rameses II.

71
72

*Plate 72 and 73*

Rameses II was the most vigorous builder of all the pharaohs and much of his construction was to his own glorification. The colossal seated statue is at Luxor; he wears the double crown of Egypt and the *uraeus* of the cobra goddess Buto. The four seated statues are all of the pharaoh, the facade of the famous rock temples at Abu Simbel before they were moved to save them from the rising waters of the Nile. The size of the statues is almost as stupendous as the pharaoh's conceit – the small figure in the upper centre is a mere god, Ra Harakhte, the guardian of the temple. Each one of the statues is sixty-five feet high.

*Plate 74*

A detail from Abu Simbel, showing the statue of the pharaoh which stands on the right of the entrance. The small figure which stands no higher than Rameses' knee is his wife Nefertari – who was also his daughter. On the side of the statue are carved the gods of the Nile.

*Plate 75*

The interior of the temple at Abu Simbel is adorned with coloured reliefs which show Rameses II in the company of the gods and goddesses. Here he is with Mut, the goddess who was the consort of Amon and who, with Khons, formed the Theban triad. It is interesting to note that the deities were always shown as resembling the pharaoh and as something like the same age. Rameses II is a young man here; no doubt the image of himself he wished to perpetuate. The gods who embrace the boy pharaoh Tutankhamun in the statues and reliefs which survive from his reign are clearly seen to be adolescent.

74
75

*Plate 76*

Nefertari had a tomb of her own – a beautiful one near present-day Luxor. The illustration shows the entrance to the sarcophagus chamber, into which a guide proceeds with his lantern. Mayet, the goddess of truth and justice, spreads her protective wings across the lintel, and the names and titles of the queen are depicted on the sides of the doors: Great Royal Wife, Mistress of the Two Lands, Nefertari.

76

*Plate 77*

A portrait of Nefertari, from her tomb.
The smaller temple at Abu Simbel is also hers, and dedicated to the goddess Hathor. The name Nefertari meant Beautiful Friend (or Companion) and the evidence suggests that she kept a permanent place in her husband's affections though she was his daughter and had been married to him before he attained the throne. Her mummy was not in the tomb when it was discovered and has never been traced. It is not known when she died.

*Plate 78*

Even when the pharaohs were no longer Egyptian they built fine temples to the country's gods. These would be dedicated to the deity in favour – the one the pharaoh believed had shown him especial grace. The Ptolemies, a dynasty of pure Greeks who ruled Egypt for nearly 300 years after the death of Alexander the Great, built two of particular interest, both of them to honour aspects of Horus. One was at Edfu on the Upper Nile, the other was even farther south, at Kom Ombo, and the ruins can be seen here, glowing in the setting sun. It was a twin sanctuary, to Horus the Elder (Haroeris) and the crocodile god Sebek.

77
78

# IV
# THE AFTERLIFE

79

*Plate 79*

A detail from the *Book of the Dead* of Ani, a scribe of the Eighteenth Dynasty.
With his wife Tutu he is shown making offerings to Osiris; the table is heaped
with fruit, bread and vegetables. Tutu carries a sistrum in one hand and wears on
her head a lotus flower, the symbol of rebirth.

The officers of the pharaoh's household were probably the only class in Egypt
who could afford elaborate tombs and many of them, especially those of the
Eighteenth Dynasty, proved to be enormously rewarding to the scholars. Ani was
probably one of the scribes of Amenophis III. The papyrus of his *Book of the Dead*
is now in the British Museum.

*Plate 80*

Osiris in the Hall of Judgment. As the supreme judge of the dead he is often shown as a mummy, either seated or standing. The Egyptians were primarily an agricultural people and like all such associated death and fertility – one was a beginning which arose out of its necessary end, the end in turn carried the seeds of another beginning. The origins of Osiris as a fertility god are remembered in the habit of portraying him with a green face. He carries the crook and flail, the twin symbols of royalty of Upper and Lower Egypt, and wears the *atef* crown. Most of our evidence for the funerary rites comes from the elaborate tombs of the powerful; nevertheless Osiris was a god for all, even the humblest, since he represented hope of another and perhaps better life after this one. Wall-painting from the tomb of Nefertari. Nineteenth Dynasty.

80

*Plate 81*

Seker, the god pictured as a sparrow-hawk, was originally a god of the dead in the religious system of the Old Kingdom with its capital at Memphis. He became identified with the Osiris cult when it spread throughout Egypt and later with Osiris himself. His original function was as the guardian of the entrance to the next world; he later became the guardian of the tomb. This representation comes from Kom Ombo during the Ptolemaic period, where he guards the sarcophagus itself.

81

*Plate 82*

As noted in other illustrations, burials took place in the west where the sun set, and this often meant a journey across the Nile. A funeral barque is depicted in this painting from the tomb of the pharaoh Seti I at Abydos. The dead man is shown as a mummy, and accompanying him is the serpent goddess Mertseger. She was known as the Mistress of the West and her name meant 'Beloved of him who makes the silence'; that is, Osiris. A desert goddess, she gave protection against the serpents of that region and was, particularly, the deity of the Theban necropolis. Nineteenth Dynasty.

82

83

*Plate 83*

The *ka* of the dead Ani. This was the transcendent part of a human being which, when he died, arose from him and travelled to the West. There the *ka* would be received by the goddess Hathor who provided refreshment, and by its heavenly self. The tomb was called the house of the *ka* and there it returned to dwell. The family of the deceased was very careful to provide nourishment for the *ka*; notwithstanding its possession of a heavenly self it was also a part of man and could perish if it lacked subsistence. In this leaf from the papyrus of Ani the *ka* is seen, left, rising from the body of the dead man and, right, at its station in the tomb.

*Plate 84*

Osiris, in the judgment hall, was attended by Isis and Nephthys and the four sons of Horus who were seated in front of his throne. Horus had numerous wives in his various aspects but these were usually believed to be his children by Isis, his mother – the Egyptians would have seen nothing wrong in that. They were appointed by their father as the guardians of the four cardinal points, and during the period when the viscera of the dead were removed during mummification they were also guardians of the jars which contained them. The human-headed Imset guarded the south and the jar containing the liver; the ape-headed Hapy guarded the north and the jar containing the lungs; falcon-headed Qebehsenuf guarded the west and the jar containing the intestines, and jackal-headed Duamutef the east and the jar containing the stomach. From the tomb of Nefertari, Nineteenth Dynasty.

84
85

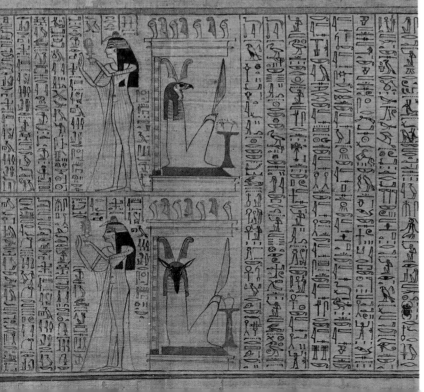

*Plate 85*

Anhai was a priestess and musician of Amon at Thebes toward the end of the Twentieth Dynasty. Her *Book of the Dead* is a beautiful and explicit document which charts the progress of the deceased Anhai to the hoped-for rebirth in the kingdom of Osiris. She would have been furnished with her *Book of the Dad* when placed in her coffin; it contained the ritual prayers that would carry her safely across the dreaded Nowhere between the living and the dead and see that she arrived safely in the Hall of Judgment. Then she would be conducted into the presence of Osiris by Anubis or Horus – Horus in this case.

*Plate 86*

When the funeral procession arrived at the tomb
the ceremony of 'The Opening of the Mouth' was
performed. This was a ritual remembrance of the
visit of Horus to his father Osiris when he was able
to take him the news that his murder had been
avenged; that Set had been defeated and the son had
attained his rightful place. In a much older tradition
it had been Set who had given the gods their power
to command – he had 'opened their mouths'.
Horus could now perform the service for his father,
which consisted of touching his lips with a
ceremonial adze. Thus was the resurrection of the
soul of Osiris achieved. The ceremony was
performed in funerals to ensure that the way was
open for the rebirth of the soul of the deceased.
From the papyrus of Hunefer, Nineteenth Dynasty.

87

*Plate 87*

In the presence of Osiris the deceased would make a declaration of purity, that he or she was never guilty of evil, and that by addressing each of the gods boldly by name could prove that they were without sin. The proceedings were recorded by the Divine Scribe, the ibis-headed god of wisdom Thoth. The illustration is from the rock temple at Abu Simbel, and the pharaoh Rameses II is shown between Ra-Harakhte, whom he is presumably addressing, and Thoth.

*Plate 88*

The protestations of the deceased were the first part of the judgment but not the part that really mattered. The first part was almost a ritual incantation, a process of declaring something firmly in the hope of making it so in fact. But the truth would have to be satisfied in the end, and here Anhai is conducted to the final test. In the Hall of Judgment was a balance, and a tall staff surmounted by the symbol of Thoth as a baboon. Ibis-headed Thoth stood ready to record the outcome, and Horus led the deceased to the last trial. The balance was kept by jackal-headed Anubis, the conductor of souls, and waiting by him stood the monster Ammut, part lion and part crocodile, the Devourer. Anubis the heart of the deceased on one side of the balance, and the figure of Mayet on the other. The heart was believed to be the seat of intelligence and if innocent of evil it would balance with truth.

88

*Plate 89*

The verdict was recorded by Thoth, who wrote the result on his tablets. If the heart and truth did not balance each other the grim monster Ammut was ready to devour the heart; that is, the deceased. If the heart was innocent of evil the goddess Mayet, seen here as a small figure in green, garlanded the deceased with the feathers of truth and they were then conducted to the throne of Osiris. Anhai is shown as having passed the crucial test, and this was not necessarily a presumption on her part. Rather it was a hope expressed.

*Plate 90*

The life in the next world that every Egyptian hoped for. On the right is Osiris, seated, and before him a ritual sacrifice. Isis and Nephthys stand behind his throne. Anhai, pure of heart, would have been offered refreshment at the request of Horus and granted the gift of living forever. Osiris would allow her to depart and mingle freely with the gods and the rest of those who enjoyed his kingdom, and assign to her a place of her own. In the centre is Anhai, about to begin her next life; she is garlanded with vine leaves. In her new world she will cherish the place assigned to her and in the centre parts of the left picture she can be seen there, enjoying what looks like pastoral bliss.

89

90

# Greek Mythology

# Introduction to
# GREEK MYTHOLOGY

Since that stage in evolution when man ceased to be an animal and became *homo sapiens*, it has been inherent in his nature, on looking at the world about him with wondering and puzzled eyes, to ask the questions 'Why?' and 'How?' It is the results of his groping attempts throughout the ages to find the answer to these questions which we call religion—or mythology: for we are inclined to consider our own beliefs—if we have any—as religion, and other people's beliefs as mythology.

A myth then is firstly, man's attempt to explain the world and the things he sees in it, and to make intelligible to himself the natural phenomena which condition his way of life in that world. His beliefs will vary according to this way of life and its needs. For example, to nomadic herdsmen, wandering about and disputing grazing territory with rival tribes, a strong, belligerent sky-god will be the best protector; while to a peaceable and settled agricultural community it is the fruitfulness of the earth-mother which is all important.

Secondly, and at a later and somewhat higher stage of human culture, a myth seeks also to justify an established social pattern together with its traditions and ritual; and it records, as it were dramatically, the historical invasions and migrations, changes of leadership and foreign influences, which combined to establish that social pattern. This second type of myth will tend to produce a hierarchy of gods which parallels the society of its believers: for instance, the gods of ancient China were members of a divine bureaucracy resembling in almost all respects the political administration of their worshippers.

At some stage in the long, slow development of these two types of myth, there will come a priest-poet, often semi-legendary, who will rationalize his people's beliefs and give a formal shape to their myth, as did Homer and Hesiod for the Greeks, and in this manner is a national religion established. And later, much later, though still based on the same primitive beginnings, will come—as they did for the Romans—the elegant sophistications of an Ovid with his *Metamorphoses*, or of an Apuleius with his charming allegory of Cupid and Psyche.

The precise difference between a myth and a folk-tale has long vexed scholars, because in many examples the theme and content of both are similar enough for their stories to be in essence the same. Just where exactly do the traditions of a people cease to be myths and become merely folk-tales? It is now generally agreed that if a story tells of a happening which affects the whole world, or all the members of a certain community, and is set at a time before a pattern of everyday life has been established, it is a myth.

*Previous.pages, left* Black figured Greek krater from early 6th century depicting Odysseus thrusting a fiery brand into Polyphemus' one eye on the island of Cyclops.

*Previous pages, right* The gold mask of the High King Agamemnon excavated from one of the royal graves at Mycenae by the great archaeologist, Schliemann.

If, on the other hand, a similar happening affects an individual living in a roughly identifiable historical or modern age, and in a setting recognizable to the hearers of the story, then it is a folk-tale.

It therefore follows that myths tell stories of the beginnings of things, and concern mainly the gods and those semi-divine culture heroes who often stand for abstract qualities—courage, kingship, warrior's strength, and so on—while folk-tales tell of individual human beings and their personal adventures, and often of anthropomorphic animals and their doings. A myth explains and rationalizes and is, for those who believe it, perpetually and repeatedly true; a folk-tale seeks only to instruct and to entertain. Thus in Jewish tradition, Adam the First Man for whom a mate was created from one of his ribs, and the Welsh solar hero Lleu whose wife Blodeuwedd was formed for him from flowers by the magician Gwydion, are part, respectively, of the Jewish and Celtic mythologies. But Cinderella's prince, wandering the land with the glass slipper in search of a particular, once-glimpsed bride is the protagonist in a folk-tale.

The myths of the ancient Greeks can be divided into three groups; firstly, myths of the Olympian gods—that is of Zeus the father-god, and of the more important of his fellow-deities; secondly, myths which explain natural phenomena; and thirdly, the hero-myths which relate the deeds and adventures of mortal heroes who were often of semi-divine parentage or ancestry, and many of whom were later deified and became numbered amongst the lesser gods of the Greek pantheon.

Greek religion followed a usual pattern of development, progressing from the simple fertility rites practised by the individual either on his own behalf or on behalf of his family, to the established state-religion with its public festivals and formalized procedures. As it developed, it shed or altered some beliefs and encompassed and adapted others. Sometimes it seemed to advance along more enlightened paths, and at other times it seemed to fall back again into a more antiquated usage, with its attendant barbarities. Yet gradually those early barbarities will have been entirely suppressed or else superceded by rites more in keeping with a higher level of culture. Religious emphasis will have varied from locality to locality; sophisticated ritual evolved more fully in the cities and larger centres of communal life; while among the primitive country folk—such as in rural Arcadia—the old superstitions and crude practices will have persisted alongside simplifications of the newer, polished forms.

The history of the development of Greek worship may be said roughly to cover, like the Christian, around 2000 years; but unlike the Christian faith Greek religion had no clear cut body of dogma, no sacred and supposedly god-inspired writings of the nature of the Jewish and Christian Bible or the Islamic Koran, and no compulsory creed, binding upon its worshippers. And this is probably why it could put up so little resistance to the spread of

Christianity: its tolerance and its respect for the adaptations and the varieties of belief of the individual were its own downfall. To the Greeks the word *hairetikos*—heretic—meant 'able to choose' and had no derogatory implication. Admittedly one of the charges brought against Socrates amounted to that of blasphemy—but then Socrates' enemies were short of ammunition and in need of every weapon, however blunt, upon which they could lay their hands. The idea of any fanatical, suppressive and persecuting religious body in the nature of the Christian Holy Office would have been not merely repugnant, but unthinkable to the Greeks, one of whose best-known maxims was 'Nothing to excess'.

Except perhaps for the later, secret, mystery cults which spread to Greece from the East, Greek faith was primarily materialistic and practical. It was a religion of everyday life unconcerned with other worldliness and the Greeks knew their deities and the accepted attributes and appearance of those deities, not through any supposed mystical experience, but through poetry and art. Poets contradicted each other in their works, as did Homer and Hesiod in some respects and art changed its style from age to age and from place to place but to the Greeks all was acceptable.

It is generally presumed today that in the prehistoric European communities, as in those of Asia Minor, Syria and Libya, the organized worship of a mother-goddess preceded that of a father-god. Man might have been taller, stronger and swifter, but it was woman who was the awe-inspiring mystery, with her strange monthly cycles, corresponding to the cycles of the moon by which man first learnt to reckon time in periods of more than a single day; it was woman who suckled and reared the young of the tribe; and above all it was woman who, alone or by the grace of some unseen supernatural power, perpetuated the race. Granted that from the moment when man first discovered the all-important truth, namely, that a child, so far from being conceived parthenogenetically, or being sired by a spirit of the wind or the waters of a stream, needs a human father for its existence, then the supreme power of woman—and with it the supreme power of the goddess—began to decline. But it was to be many ages before the Great Goddess was forced to yield her foremost position to the father-god. And in the ancient world she was never entirely ousted, never relegated to a place of no importance. In Greece, the protector and patron of Athens, even at the height of its political and military glory was the goddess Athene; and even in historical times there were religious festivals exclusive to women, such as the Thesmophoria, celebrated in Attica during the month of October, from which men were forbidden—a situation which the dramatist Aristophanes, in his *Thesmophoriazusae* uses to such splendidly ribald comic advantage.

Early in the second millennium BC the Hellenic invasions of mainland Greece began. At first they will have been

on a small scale and far less destructive than those which followed them. These early so-called Aeolian and Ionian invasions were probably little more than the infiltration of armed bands of nomadic herdsmen who pressed southwards in search of a more settled existence. They probably spoke an early form of Indo-European language and worshipped the Aryan trinity of sky-gods, Indra, Varuna and Mitra. After initial skirmishes, they will no doubt have settled down peaceably enough and intermarried with the pre-Hellenic agricultural peoples whom they found in Thessaly and central Greece: and their gods will have been accepted by these goddess-worshipping farmers as new children of the Mother.

After the Aeolian and Ionian invasions the more destructive and far reaching Achaean and Dorian invasions as they are called came from the north. This time the invaders were larger bands of experienced warriors rather than herdsmen and peaceable settlement and intermarriage were less to their liking than conquest and appropriation of territory and the slaughter or enslavement of those whose lands they invaded. The initial uneasy relationship between conquering invaders and conquered native inhabitants, might still be observed unchanged in classical times in Sparta, where the pre-Dorian population had been entirely enslaved and formed the Helots, an unprivileged class which performed all menial tasks and was utterly subservient to the ruling warrior class, by whom it was never assimilated.

At a time when the Greek mainland was still in a state of barbarism, there was already a flourishing and mainly peaceable civilization on the island of Crete, with strong trade connections with the East and in particular with Egypt. This civilization is known as Minoan from the name of its legendary founder, King Minos. Around 1600 BC its influence spread to the mainland, having its strongest effect in Argolis, where it resulted in the so-called Mycenaean civilization, centred around the town of Mycenae. In about 1400 BC the Minoan civilization on Crete collapsed probably as the result of a natural disaster—an earthquake, or the eruption of a volcano—which was followed by a successful invasion from the mainland of a powerful army which took full advantage of the chaos and disorganization brought about by the recent disaster.

The history of the development of Greek religion shows it to have been influenced by beliefs from many other lands, including Babylonia, Egypt, Palestine and Phrygia but it is in Crete that its true beginnings are to be found. There, as elsewhere, the first forms of worship will have been the veneration of natural objects such as rocks, trees and animals; and of stylizations of certain man-made objects of vital importance to man's survival such as weapons, the hearth, a supporting roof-pillar and so on. The chief amongst these cult objects will have survived into the period of anthropomorphic deities to become attributes or symbols of the deities.

In Crete the special survivals were the Minoan doubleheaded axe, now well known from its many representations in Cretan art; the bull, a symbol of virility in several religions; the dove, a bird much given to mating-display and therefore associated with fertility; and the snake which periodically sloughs its skin and may from this be said to annually reborn. The snake in particular became much venerated in Greece in the classical period: and to this very day in certain country districts it is the subject of reverent superstition amongst the Greek peasants. Votive statuettes from shrines and tombs in Crete and depictions in art of these three creatures and of the doubleheaded axe are common, so also are the numerous representations of the Cretan Great Goddess in her several forms. Probably one of the best-known figurines from the ancient world is that statue of the so-called Minoan snake-goddess—the Great Goddess, or her priestess, dressed as a fashionable Cretan lady with bared breasts and flounced skirt, holding one of her sacred snakes in either hand.

Though something may be conjectured, we know little of the actual practices of Cretan religion or of its myths other than what has survived in an adapted form in later Hellenic practices. We do not even know the names of the Great Goddess, though one of them, in her aspect as Mother, was probably Rhea; and as the springtime Maiden she seems to have sometimes been called Britomartis. But under whatever names she was worshipped she will undoubtedly have been at first, all-powerful and revered throughout Crete in her three aspects as Maiden, Mother and Old Woman and she presided in one or other of her three forms, over every phase of human life and every occurrence in the daily round.

The pattern of annual worship in early Crete will probably have been similar to that offered to the Great Goddess in every place where she was supreme. She was represented by her high priestess, whose chosen consort was the father of the child which she bore annually—her fruitfulness being both the outward sign of the goodwill of the goddess towards the worshippers, and an encouraging reminder to the fields to give good yield that year, and to the flocks and herds to multiply. At first this consort will have been slain annually and replaced by a successor, probably at seed-sowing time when the sacrificed consort's blood and the pieces of his body will have been sprinkled and scattered on the fields to fertilize them.

From place to place the method will have varied by which the consort was slain: but on mainland Greece and in some localities of Asia Minor we can guess at it from clues given in myths concerning local deities and heroes who will, originally, have been consorts of the goddess. For instance, in Mysia the consort, like Hylas was drowned; in Thrace he was torn in pieces by the women worshippers or the priestesses, as was Orpheus; around Mount Ida in Asia Minor where the Great Goddess was worshipped as Cybele, we can tell that he was bled to death from the fate of Attis; and in Elis he was probably flung from a moving chariot, as was Oeno-

maus. We cannot be sure how he was slain in Crete, but perhaps he was despatched by means of the doubleheaded axe.

Gradually the position of the consort will have increased in importance. There will have been occasions during his year of office when, wearing the sacred robes of the goddess-priestess and temporarily invested with her magical power, he will have acted as her understudy. Also as time went on, it became the custom to kill each year not last year's consort, but a youth chosen in his place. And so from these adaptations and variations of earlier practice, will have arisen the first concept of kingship.

In Crete the Great Goddess's consort—the corn-youth, the priest-king, the dying-god—was from early times associated with the bull, an association which owed much to influence from the bull-cults of the East, such as those of Sumeria and Elam. Later, after the destruction of Minoan power, this Cretan bull-god was equated with Zeus, the sky-god from the mainland, and his attributes were assimilated with those of the newcomer. The fact that Zeus, supreme god of the Greek pantheon in later times, was originally a fusion of two important gods (for a moment we may here disregard the many minor, local mainland deities whose cults were swallowed up by his) is clearly displayed by the divergence of sites claimed as his birthplace. These sites include Arcadia, Messenia and Olympia—this last claim being made in a tradition which offers an explanation of the founding of the Olympic Games. But none of these mainland sites has the importance of Crete, from where comes a full and detailed version of the story of his birth as the son of Rhea—one of the Great Goddess's names as Mother. 'Cretanborn' was a stock epithet of Zeus. Moreover, if further proof is needed that Zeus, who became the immortal, never-aging, supreme god of historical times, was once the annually-dying consort of the Great Goddess, it is offered by the existence of the several sites revered as his burial-place, both on Crete—at Knossos and at Mount Dicte—and on the mainland.

After the fall of Crete, the leadership of the Aegean world passed to Mycenae in Argolis, where a culture very different from that of Crete had grown up over the years, though it had originally owed much to Cretan influence. Compared with Knossos, that splendid, largely unfortified Cretan city, with its peaceable, luxurious way of life and its pre-eminent Great Goddess, Mycenae was little more than a huge armed fortress of god-worshipping warriors, lead by a strong priest-king.

The power of the Great Goddess was now everywhere being superceded by the power of the god. But she did not surrender without a fight. Those myths which tell of the too-frequent quarrels between Zeus and Hera, his sister and queen, may appear undignified to us at first sight, but are simply allegories of the struggle between the old worship and the new—as indeed, are most myths which tell of divine revolts. Similarly, the tales of Zeus's numerous amorous adventures that are linked with specific

districts in so many parts of Greece, are a euphemistic statement of the old enforced 'marriage' between the conquering god and the local form of the Great Goddess—a union which, in many cases, will actually have taken place between the war-leader of the victorious invaders and the queen or high priestess of the captured district.

Also at about this time the old system of matrilineal succession died out and its place was taken by the custom of the invaders—a son now succeeded his father and no longer, as under the old order, left his father's home to marry into the family of his bride. Instead it was she who left her father's house and went to live in the house of her husband's father; while it was her brother who inherited the lands and rights which would, in earlier days, have been hers and her husband's. But in many myths the old order lives on. To mention but one of these; Menelaus leaves Argolis to go to Sparta where he marries Helen, the (supposed) daughter of the King, and in due time becomes himself the ruler of Sparta by virtue of his marriage. Small wonder then, one might think, that he so readily forgave Helen's adultery! An example of later custom is seen in the marriage of one of Helen's unsuccessful suitors, Odysseus. Rejected by Helen he woos Penelope, the daughter of a Spartan chieftain and in spite of her father's objections, persuades her to leave Sparta and go with him to his own home on the island of Ithaca.

Gradually, over the centuries there evolved a similar pattern of worship for all Greece, and a pantheon of deities was established, though inevitably divergencies and inconsistencies remained for all the efforts of the ancient poets and mythographers who sought to explain and reconcile them.

Foremost in this Greek pantheon in historical times were the so-called Twelve Olympians—the elite amongst the gods and goddesses. They were believed to dwell with Zeus, their lord—and for some of them, their father—in palaces surrounding his stronghold on Mount Olympus, though they did not always live in amity with him. Now and then one or another of them, including Hera, his queen, would rebel against his authority. This situation was a reflection of the conditions prevailing in earlier times since in just the same manner did the chieftains of a king sometimes challenge his authority; and the lesser kings of Greece flout the leadership of the high King Agamemnon in Homer's *Iliad*.

The list of the Twelve Olympians was modified from time to time, but they are most frequently given as Zeus, Poseidon, Hera, Demeter, Apollo, Artemis, Aphrodite, Ares, Hephaestus, Hermes, Athene and Hestia. Latterly Hestia was usually replaced by the important newcomer from Thrace, Dionysus.

In spite of that deposition, however, Hestia was highly revered by all as a very ancient and important aspect of the Great Goddess. The hearth where she was believed to preside was the very heart of the home, and was moreover, like the altar of a medieval church, a safe asylum where a suppliant might beg the protection of the householder. Sacred oaths were sworn by her name and since she was not only the fire of the hearth, but also the sacred fire of the temple altar, the first portion of every sacrifice was offered to Hestia. In most towns she had her public sanctuary with its own hearth fire from which emigrant Greeks, setting off to found a colony, would carry embers to kindle the sacred fire in their new home.

Just as Greek mythology has been affected and modified by cults from other lands, so the most important of the Greek gods exerted a strong influence on both the gods of the Roman pantheon and the earlier, native Etruscan deities. The chief Roman gods in their latest forms are usually equated with the Twelve Olympians. In western Europe from the time of the Renaissance, when there was an immense revival of interest in classical art and learning, until comparatively recently the deities of Greece have been referred to by the names of their Roman counterparts (except by Greek scholars). And even today, though we may differentiate between the two groups of deities and call the gods of Greece by their own Greek names, we still latinize the spelling. For the convenience of any reader to whom the Roman gods are more familiar than those of Greece, the principal deities (and one famous hero) of both mythologies are listed here, each one named being paired with his or her counterpart.

| *Greek* | *Roman* |
|---------|---------|
| Zeus | Jupiter |
| Poseidon | Neptune |
| Hades | Pluto |
| Hera | Juno |
| Demeter | Ceres |
| Persephone | Proserpina |
| Hestia | Vesta |
| Apollo | Apollo |
| Artemis | Diana |
| Aphrodite | Venus |
| Eros | Cupid |
| Ares | Mars |
| Hephaestos | Vulcan |
| Hermes | Mercury |
| Dionysus | Bacchus |
| Asklepios | Aesculapius |
| Heracles | Hercules |

There were sceptics and atheists amongst the intellectuals, but to the average Greek of the classical period, as to his ancestors, the gods were present everywhere, though unseen. In

appearance they were thought of as being like men, only far more beautiful and with infinitely nobler minds, and that is how they were depicted in art—idealized and perfect. As well as being more beautiful the gods were immeasurably more skilled than their worshippers. Indeed, over whatsoever craft or skill—artistic, domestic, military or any other—a deity presided, he was unquestionably the greatest of all the practitioners of that craft or skill. If a man possessed any talent or rejoiced in any measure of skill it was reckoned as a gift from the gods and therefore the Greeks believed it fitting that he should not waste it, but use it to the best of his ability, so that he might, in a modest way, resemble the gods themselves. However, it was imperative that it should only be in a modest way, since to think oneself too like a god was to offend against the gods and to be guilty of *hubris*—reckless pride. Once again that favourite Greek maxim admonishes: 'Nothing to excess'.

Just as their beauty and their skills were far beyond any to which a man might attain, so the gods were also above the restrictions which governed human behaviour and were not expected to follow the rules of conduct which had been laid down for man. This attitude to divine morality prevailed largely unchanged throughout the whole age during which the Greek gods were worshipped. Even at the latest period, when high standards of human morality had long replaced the early unenlightened ways, the gods were still not expected to conform; and in the popular conception only two gods developed to show any ethical improvement in attributes and characteristics. These two were Zeus and Apollo, the two deities who had the strongest influence on every sphere and aspect of Greek life and thought. Because they believed their gods to be everywhere and in everything, and because they were bound by no inflexible dogmas or doctrines, the Greeks found no difficulty in reconciling science and religion. All scientific discoveries were merely attributed to the Gods' powers.

Though the Greeks felt reverence for their gods, they could laugh at them as well and see no sin in it. As early as Homer they were laughing—the Homeric *Hymn to Hermes* contains humourous anecdotes of some of Hermes' merry pranks—and in the *Iliad*, Homer makes several of the gods and goddesses look very foolish indeed on the battlefield, when they interfere in the conduct of the war. In later literature there are frequent divine appearances in drama. Often the god enters only towards the end of the action—as the original *deus ex machina*, in fact—and resolves the difficulties of the protagonists and closes the drama on a suitably uplifting note. But sometimes he plays a longer and more important role—and a role, moreover, which is not always dignified. It is hard to recognize the beautiful and rather terrifying young Dionysus of the *Bacchae* of Euripides when we meet him again as a figure of fun in the *Frogs* of the comic poet Aristophanes—who was no liberal-minded 'modern' like Euripides, but an unashamed reactionary who hankered after the good old days. If we worshipped Dionysus, the divine protector of theatres and the deity who presided over dramatic art, we would hardly dare to show him as an absurd, cowardly dilettante, with less dignity than his own slave. Yet it is all very entertaining and laughable, and the Greeks saw no blasphemy in it.

In their towns and cities the Greeks worshipped their gods in the beautiful temples which they built to honour them —most often on some ancient hallowed site. Though any individual might approach any of the gods on his own behalf, by archaic and classical times worship was principally communal and public. The most elaborate rites and ceremonies were those observed by the state on behalf of all the people; but each small township, as well as every local clan or family of importance, also had its own particular observances.

Human sacrifice was abandoned in Greece as unworthy and degrading from about the sixth century BC, though animals continued to be offered to the gods, as well as fruits and flowers. An integral part of the public religious ceremonies was a solemn procession through the streets of the city to the temple of victims and objects sacred to the deity concerned. There, with hymns and prayers—often written by the most famed and respected poets and musicians of the day—the victims would be sacrificed in an elaborate and orderly ritual, and the ceremony would end with the worshippers partaking of a feast of the flesh of the sacrificed animals.

These public, civic cults were fixed according to a state calendar and though many of them were connected with the vital affairs of agriculture, through the years they had come to be celebrated on days which did not always correspond with the real seasons of the farming year. This was not so much the case in country districts where, then as now, work was ruled by weather conditions and the harvest was celebrated at the time of its gathering.

From around the end of the fifth century BC the cult of a latecomer to the Greek pantheon—Asklepios, the god of medicine—grew in popularity. The swift advance of his worship coincided with a development in philosophical ideas about the importance of the individual; and even those thinkers who were inclined to feel sceptical towards the Olympian deities paid respect to the gentle healer and acknowledged the worth of his cult. By Christian times his worship was widespread and strong and of all the gods of the Greeks, Asklepios was the only one whose cult presented any danger to the march of Christianity. As paganism was crushed out, yet still the loyal worshippers of Asklepios resisted, while many of his shrines were appropriated and given to wonder-working Christian saints. And thus, not quite everything that was good in the religion of the Greeks was lost and destroyed by the intolerance of monotheism; a little—albeit a very little— was for a time preserved to bring comfort to men.

*Barbara Leonie Picard*

# I
# BEFORE THE OLYMPIANS

1

*Plate 1*

The southern gateway of the palace of Knossos, with the horns of consecration.
The Minoan culture of Crete saw the Aegean civilization at its highest point:
the many currents had mingled for thousands of years before this remarkable
flowering. The archaeologists have shown how much the concept of the
Earth Goddess—the Mother—dominated the religious practices of the Greek
people in ancient times; the serpent and bull symbols which recur so frequently
in connection with her in Knossos are both expressions of fertility and man
came to realize very early that without her goodwill he might have no harvest, no
fruitfulness. She was still propitiated even when alien gods seemed to have
usurped her place.

**Plate 2**

A group of marble figures from the island of
Naxos. They date from about 2,500 BC and
are typical of the many pieces commonly called
Cycladic, from the group of islands of which
Naxos is one. Their great antiquity combines with
a lack of evidence to invest them with mystery—it is
impossible to determine exactly what they were.
Loosely referred to as idols or fertility figures, their
chief interest lies in the fact that legend connects the
Cyclades with Crete: the islands were said to have
been ruled by the Carians, who were driven out
by Minos, King of Crete. The Carians were
from Asia Minor, and the features common to all
religions of the eastern Mediterranean were to some
extent due to the exchange of ideas.

2

**Plate 3**

A primitive vase found in a tomb at Koumasi in
Crete. It is probably from the same period as the
Cycladic figures but here an attempt has been made
to express a positive idea. The serpent was an
ancient symbol of fertility and renewal and therefore
an apt symbol for the Mother. It was also a sexual
symbol, being at once phallic and a swallower.
In this crude representation a snake is draped over
the shoulders of a female figure.

3                                                    4

**Plate 4**

Here is the same idea, but presented by the
sophisticated Cretans at the height of the Minoan
culture, between the eighteenth and fifteenth
centuries BC. This beautiful terracotta figurine is
thought by some to represent a serpent goddess
but it is more likely to be the figure of a priestess.
That she serves the Mother is seen by the snakes
twined round her arms, while the conical
headdress suggests that she is dressed for a ceremony.
The rest of her costume was common to the
ladies of the court of Knossos; they are all seen, in
both statuettes and wall paintings, to be wearing
gowns which lie open at the top to give full
exposure to the breasts; the gowns are all tightly
waisted and fall in flounces to the ankles.

5

*Plate 5*

The bull-leaping fresco from the palace of Knossos.
The sport looks dangerous—seizing the horns and
somersaulting over the bull's back would
require remarkable timing and a high degree
of fitness. But games in Crete (if this was indeed
a game) probably occurred at festivals, as they did
in Greece, and the bull symbol is ubiquitous in
the art of the Cretans. Like the serpent it was an
important cult animal; it also expressed fertility but
added the quality of strength. The story of
Theseus and the Minotaur—the offspring of a queen
who mated with a bull—took place in Crete.

*Plate 6*

A ritual vase in the shape of a bull's head carved
from black steatite and inlaid with rock crystal
and shell. It is a fine example of the Minoan art of
the fifteenth century BC. With a mother goddess
in the supreme position it was inevitable that
her consort should be expressed as the embodiment
of male strength and creative energy. It was
probably from this association that the myth of
Theseus and the Minotaur grew; the later
Greeks did not give the myths their form until many
centuries had passed, and they connected Crete and
the figure of Theseus with a heroic age. The
gods they honoured were rather human and like
themselves—not the expression of natural
forces imperfectly understood and therefore to be
feared and respected. Theseus, one of their great
ancestors, would not have been honoured if he had
crossed the seas to fight a mere man; the bull
motif would have provided the Greeks'
imagination with a monster, and their hero with a
worthy adversary.

7

*Plate 7*

The bull as a sacrifice. From the Minoan site at Hagia Triada comes this sarcophagus, carved from a block of limestone and covered with white plaster on which scenes from the funeral rites were painted. This one shows the sacrifice of a bull which was bound and laid on the altar; a priestess stands on the left and a musician plays in the background. The blood will drain into the vessel at the foot of the altar. The coffin dates from about the fifteenth century BC.

8

9

*Plate 8 and 9*

There is ample evidence that mainland Greece was familiar with the customs and beliefs of Crete— indeed at this time in history it is likely that they were widespread in the Aegean. This gold cup was found in a royal tomb at Vaphio, south of Sparta. It is Cretan work and shows the capture of bulls, probably wild ones. They might be for use in the arena for the bull-leaping game, or for sacrifice, or simply for breeding. Above a bull has been netted and thrown. Left it is being hobbled by a hunter who wears the long hair and tightly-waisted kilt familiar from the frescoes at Knossos. The cup dates from the sixteenth century BC, when the Mycenean culture was beginning to grow in strength. Later it would completely overcome the Minoan.

# II
# THE COMING OF ORDER

10

*Plate 10*

Little is known for certain about the gods of the Greeks in the dark centuries that
followed the destruction of the Minoan culture. The Indo-European
migrations were bringing new men down into the peninsula in the early part
of the second millennium and a new, male-orientated society was mingling with
the old. The Achaeans—those described by Homer—came in the thirteenth
century BC; they were warlike and ruthless and the tide seemed to be irreversible.
A god-king challenged the Mother. Tradition, however, dies hard, and the new
All-powerful was given a childhood in Crete. The picture shows the cave of
Dicte, on the Aegean Hill, where Rhea, the mother of Zeus, hid her son from his
father Cronus.

11

12

13

*Plate 11*

The shaft graves at Mycenae. Towards the end of the second millennium the Achaeans were followed by the Dorians; a usurper race was in fact displaced by one even more powerful though adhering to much the same religious ideas. Sky-gods replaced the Mother in all parts of Greece, a process often brought about by the taking of wives from the old ruling clans, and imposing a new religion together with a new order. But it was by no means a peaceful process; and the troubled world to which the Homeric heroes returned after the fall of Troy is probably a reflection of this.

*Plate 12*

The castration of Uranus. The stories of the gods and their beginnings were given a definite shape by Homer and Hesiod, and were generally accepted by the eighth and seventh centuries BC. Ge, or Mother Earth, emerged from Chaos and bore Uranus, the starry universe, who became her consort. All their children were hated by Uranus who feared any challenge to his rule, and the Titans, the Giants, the Cyclops and Cronus were confined to the nether world. The angry Earth Mother released her youngest son, Cronus, and encouraged him to castrate his father and rule in his place.

*Plate 13*

The peak of Mount Olympus. When Cronus succeeded to his father's place he took his sister Rhea as his consort. (Interestingly, Rhea was probably the name by which the Mother was known in Crete.) Warned by Ge that one of his children would destroy him, he followed his father and swallowed his children as soon as they were born. The enraged Rhea gave him a stone to swallow in place of his third son, Zeus, whom she hid until he reached manhood. Zeus then enlisted the help of Cyclops, Giants, some of the Titans (including Prometheus) and waged war on Cronus and the rest of the Titans from Mount Olympus. Zeus was victorious; Cronus disappeared from myth and the stage was set for the ordering of the gods and their place in the consciousness of the Greeks. Even Zeus was insecure to begin with though he was eventually to rule unchallenged.

*Plate 14*

The great archaeologist Schliemann undertook the excavation of Mycenae which was the seat of the High King Agamemnon and the gold mask is from one of the royal graves. When Schliemann lifted it he saw for a brief moment the face of a fair-bearded king, before it crumbled to dust. He sent a telegram to the King of Greece: 'I have gazed upon the face of Agamemnon.' It is certain now that the fair-bearded king will never be identified and there is no way of ascertaining who he was. But the intense drama of that moment in the grave is easy to imagine.

15

*Plate 15*

One of the challenges that Zeus and the other
Olympians had to face was the rebellion of
the Giants who were born to Ge when the blood of
the castrated Uranus fell on her. A detail from the
frieze of the Syphian treasury at Delphi shows one of
the Giants attacked by a lion—the creature of
Cybele. Cybele was an Asiatic goddess from the
Near East, the Great Mother, and identified by the
Greeks with Rhea. Her cult found its way to
Greece by way of the Greeks of Phrygia, in
Asia Minor.

*Plate 16*

Prometheus in Greek mythology is not only man's
first friend; in some traditions he is also his
creator, having fashioned him from clay and
breathed life into him. Prometheus learned much
from Athene, at whose birth he assisted, and
he passed his knowledge on to mankind.
His benefactions to man were a source of Zeus'
wrath, which was further aroused by the
knowledge that Prometheus possessed a secret that
could end his supremacy. He ordered that
Prometheus be chained to a rock in the Caucusus,
and every day sent an eagle to feed on his liver,
which was resored each succeeding night; the
torture would thus be perpetual.

17

*Plate 17*

The secret that only Prometheus knew was that Zeus, who could not control his lusts, would one day seduce the nereid, Thetis. Any son of Thetis would prove to be greater than his father—and Zeus would fall. Eventually the two were reconciled: Prometheus told Zeus the secret, and Zeus granted him the immortality that the centaur, Chiron, was longing to surrender. Chiron was suffering from an incurable wound but being immortal could never die and find release from pain. Prometheus was possibly a fire god in origin; but the struggle with Zeus serves to underline the rejection of the former way of things—there were to be no more challenges to the king of the gods. Prometheus is one of the most interesting figures in Greek mythology, and the central figure in one of the tragedies of Aeschylus who presents him as the personification of man's eternal resistance to arbitrary fate. In this fourth-century Corinthian terracotta Thetis is seen riding a sea-horse, and carrying the helmet of Achilles—whose mother she was to become, though not by Zeus.

18

*Plate 18*

Zeus and another challenge. He is about to engage in combat with the monster Typhon. The son of Ge, he challenged the sky god, and the sight of him struck terror into the hearts of the other Olympians, who disguised themselves as animals and fled. Zeus got much the worst part of the opening struggle; Typhon severed the sinews of his hands and feet and left him lying helpless in a cave. He was rescued by Hermes and Pan, and his sinews restored. He was eventually victorious, and Zeus buried Typhon under Mount Etna which still heaves and belches smoke with the struggles of the monster within. Painting on a water jar, sixth century BC.

# III
# THE OLYMPIANS

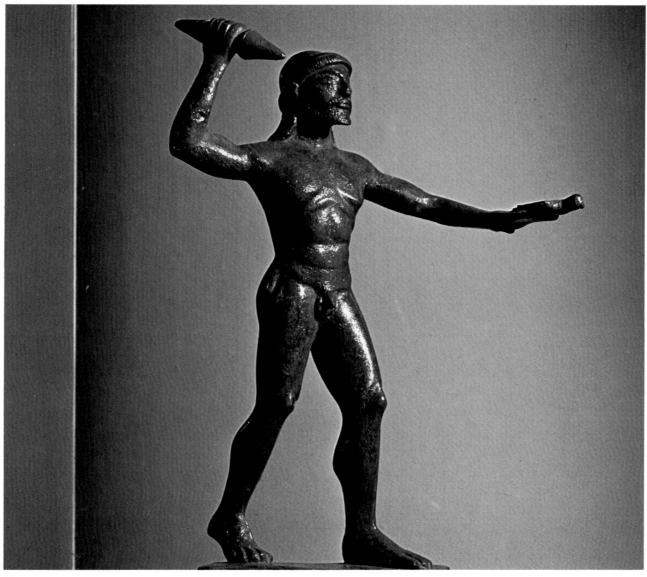

19

*Plate 19*

A Greek bronze of Zeus bearing a thunderbolt. As the sky god he is the embodiment of an idea which was ancient long before the Dorians found their way down into Greece, and can be definitely identified in the religion of ancient India. He was originally the Indo-European *weather* god as well—he who controlled the thunder and the rain, a deity of the first importance to migratory herdsmen. The third son of Cronus according to Hesiod, he is made the first son by Homer, who also describes the division of the world among the three sons: Poseidon was given the seas and Hades the underworld; Zeus himself retained the heavens. He ruled by the counsel of Ge—through all the changes in Greek religion the Mother remained. She could both foretell the future and act as the instrument of fate. The bronze is fifth-century and comes from Dodona, where there was an oracle of Zeus.

20

*Plate 20*

The most famous temple of Zeus in classical Greece was the one at Olympia—not, as might be supposed, somewhere near Mount Olympus; Olympia was in Elis, in the Peloponnese. The Olympic Games were held there, every fourth year, and in the sacred precinct were two temples, one to Hera and a magnificent one to Zeus. It was 220 feet long and 90 feet wide; the columns were 30 feet high. Next to Delphi Olympia was the greatest religious centre of Greece. It retained its position until the fourth century AD, when the Emperor Theodosius, a Christian, issued an edict enjoining the destruction of all pagan sites.

*Plate 21*

Zeus enthroned. This impressive marble statue shows him as ruler and father. He was the dispenser of good and evil in the fortunes of men, and the giver of laws that ruled the course of events. He had many titles: defender of the house, defender of the hearth, upholder of the right to liberty, maintainer of the laws of hospitality, guardian of property. He was also *Chthonios*, the god of the earth and the giver of fertility, a title which showed the persistence of the connection in Greek minds of the male god as a consort. Despite the extraordinary virtues which were uttered in his praise Zeus was, paradoxically, a very human god. His rages were accepted as natural bad temper and his casual disregard of marriage laws no obstacle to an acceptance of him as both lawgiver and *paterfamilias*. His love affairs with members of both sexes were the subject of comedy and his treatment of Prometheus seen as a regrettable stage in the establishment of order.

## Plate 22

The marriage of Zeus and Hera, from the fifth-century temple at Selinunte. Hera was one of the children of Cronus and Rhea and thus sister as well as wife to Zeus. Her character in Greek mythology is not attractive and her moments of angry spite were almost always caused through jealousy of her husband's amours. Certainly he was wayward enough to test the most patient wife but the many stories of his infidelities can be traced to something more than mere lustfulness. The ascendancy of the god, as opposed to the goddess with whom the native Greeks had been familiar for centuries, was often accomplished by the union of a local deity with the newcomer —and the object of his lust can often be identified in this way. Since many royal houses claimed descent from him his extra-marital adventures were also required to cover a very wide field.

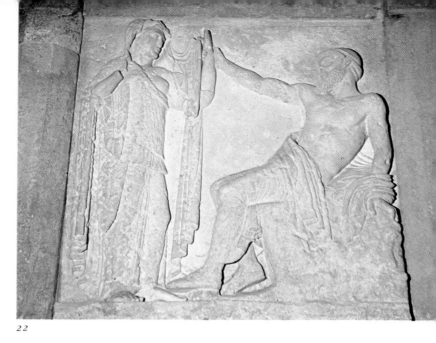

22

## Plate 23

One of the loves of Zeus was Europa, the daughter of Agenor, King of Tyre. She used to walk with her companions near the seashore, and one day she noticed a beautiful white bull among her father's cattle. She hung garlands on his horns and then climbed on his back—whereupon the bull plunged into the sea and swam away with her. He carried her to the island of Crete and took his pleasure of her there, and the children of this union were Minos, Rhadamanthus and Sarpedon. The reigning king of Crete, Asterius, married Europa and having no sons of his own adopted hers. The connections with Crete in the myth is interesting as it raises the factor of the bull cult. Europa is seen here on a sixth-century vase painting from Caere.

23

24

## Plate 24

Zeus in the guise of a swan pays court to Leda—an affair which was to have serious consequences. She was the daughter of Thestios, King of Aetolia and the wife of Tyndareus, King of Sparta. Leda liked to bathe in the river Eurotas, where one day she saw a swan swimming beside her. The swan being Zeus, the sequel was inevitable— though Leda must have been rather disconcerted to find herself laying eggs as the result of her dalliance. However, Tyndareus lay with her that night too and there is no record in the myths that he found his wife's way of bearing children unusual. Three children emerged from the egg: Castor and Pollux, and the beautiful Helen.

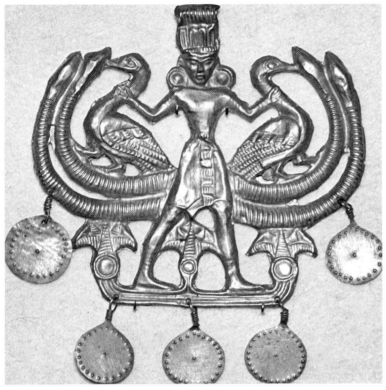

25

26

*Plate 25*

The story of Leda and the swan may have arisen from a memory of a nature cult; they were familiar in Greece and Crete in early times. This gold pendant is from Aegina but the workmanship is Cretan. A god or a priest is standing on a lotus plant, holding a swan in each hand. *c* 2,000 BC.

*Plate 26*

Hera was the legitimate consort of Zeus and occupied first place among the goddesses of the Greeks. Homer describes her as 'Argive' Hera, a reference to the origin of her cult in Argos. Her character was formidable and there is good reason to see her as the survival of a powerful cult of the Mother in Argos—marrying her was perhaps the only way open to Zeus of reconciling his power with hers: that is to say that the new Greeks found this way of reconciling the original people with themselves; Hera, as Mother, would have had no consort at all or else one of little importance. The patron and guardian of marriage, Hera also watched over women in childbirth and her blessing was sought to bring fruitfulness to the womb. She makes a striking appearance in the myth of the Argonauts as the befriender of Jason against his enemy Pelias; Pelias had withheld his homage to the goddess—a dangerous thing to do where Hera was concerned. In this Attic red-figured vase she is seen with Hebe, her daughter by Zeus who was cup-bearer to the gods.

*Plate 27*

Hera's temple at Agrigento, the ancient Acragas. Acragas was on the south-west coast of Sicily, an island popular with emigrant Greeks throughout their history. The city prospered through its trade with Carthage and built superb temples in the classical style; the poet Pindar in particular was lavish in his praise. The city, which was founded in the sixth century BC, was sacked by the Carthaginians during one of their conflicts with Rome in 405.

28

*Plate 28*

Hera gives the charge of the winds to Aeolus. Zeus himself found the winds a troublesome responsibility; they might, when his attention was diverted, have blown both earth and sea away. He confined them within a cliff that floated in the Tyrrhenian Sea among some islands, and to those islands Aeolus sailed in search of a home. That the bestowal of the winds on Aeolus should have been the action of Hera is explained by one authority in terms of Hera's original character as the Mother: the winds were her messengers. Delacroix's painting is distinctly Romantic in tone but the figure of Aeolus, after whom the Aeolian islands were named, has the appropriate heroic look.

29

*Plate 29*

Poseidon, the brother of Zeus and the lord of the seas. He was also, and probably more significantly, the god chiefly connected with horses, which suggests that his origin was very ancient indeed and dated from the time of the migrations. (The importance of the sea to the Greeks came much later.) The horse was a creature of enormous importance to the Indo-European migrants; it provided transport, food, clothing and was a visible symbol of fertility. Poseidon's title, *Hippios*, identifies him firmly and the horse appears again and again in the traditions of the Greeks. When Greek religion was formalized the ancient deity was probably given the domain that seemed closest to his original character, following the ancient idea that river (water) gods were horses and the symbolism of the white crests of the waves. Poseidon was not, apparently, content with his portion; he squabbled with Athene for the possession of Attica and with Hera for that of Aegina.

*Plate 30*

A marble group from Smyrna, dating from the second century AD. The sculpture is notable not only for its late date but also because it actually shows Poseidon and Demeter together. The myth concerning them is very strange and probably a confusion of several different stories. Poseidon lusted after Demeter (his sister according to Hesiod) but she would have none of him, grieving as she was over her lost daughter Persephone. To escape his attentions Demeter turned herself into a mare, and slipped in among the horse herds of Arcadia. However her transformation had not escaped the keen eye of Poseidon; he promptly turned himself into a stallion and joined the herd too. The furious Demeter soon found herself mounted by a triumphant Poseidon. The offspring of this remarkable coupling was the magical horse, Arion, who became the property of Adrastus, King of Argos.

30

*Plate 31*

Poseidon's temple on the promontory at Sounion, the cape which forms the southern tip of Attica. The cape was a welcome landmark for the Athenian sailors making for the Piraeus and there was a temple to Poseidon under construction which was destroyed by the Persians before it could be completed. The columns which survive are from the marble temple to the god of the seas built by the Athenians in the late fifth century BC. It was at Cape Sounion that Apollo struck down Menelaus' pilot on the voyage back from Sparta. Menelaus was delayed and his brother Agamemnon, returning alone to Mycenae, fell victim to Clytemnestra and Aegisthus.

31

*Plate 32*

Demeter, the goddess who more than any other personified for the Greeks the timeless idea of the fruitful earth. She was an ancient deity of mainland Greece, the corn-goddess on whom survival depended. In later times she is also the sorrowing mother of Persephone who was abducted by Hades, the god of the underworld. Her anguished search for her daughter led her to neglect the earth and it ceased to be fruitful: Zeus had to intervene lest the earth became completely barren and mankind perished. She was at Eleusis when her daughter was restored to her, and the Mysteries of her cult were celebrated there: those and the great festival of the Thesmophoria (of Demeter Thesmophoros— the bringer of treasures) were the most popular and widely attended of all Greek religion. Demeter as the sorrowing mother is strikingly portrayed in this marble of the fourth century BC.

32

33

34

35

*Plate 33*

Demeter and Kore. This vase painting shows mother and daughter (*kore*—maiden) with ears of corn. 'The maiden' was another way of referring to Persephone and this lends weight to the opinion that she was simply another aspect of the same goddess. The ancient Mother was in some respects the eternal woman—the mother who bore the maiden, who became a mother, who later attended on other births, who laid out the dead, who died herself, who was renewed as the maiden, who became a mother. . . . The myth relates how Persephone, at the intervention of Zeus, would have been permanently returned by Hades; but she had eaten the food of the dead— four pomegranate seeds—and was really bound to Hades for ever. In the end the god of the underworld exacted a price for her release: for each of the seeds she ate she would have to spend a month with him. This was agreed: each year Persephone returns to Hades, and winter falls upon the land.

*Plate 34*

Hades, seen with Persephone on a Greek amphora found in Apulia. He was the brother of Zeus, Poseidon, and Demeter also; Hesiod's arrangement of the family of the Olympians makes him a lustful uncle. To the Greeks he was the ruler of the world of the dead and they also gave this name to his realm, which was separated from the world of the living by the river Styx. The dead were ferried across by Charon, whose fee for the service was placed in the mouth of the corpse. The burial rites were therefore all-important. At the entrance to Hades stood the watch-dog Cerberus, who prevented those who entered from ever leaving again. Hades helped in the defeat of Cronus by stealing his weapons, and while not regarded with affection by the Greeks he exacted a great deal of respect. But he was not a *punisher*—the Greeks had no conception of any god who might be equated with Satan.

*Plate 35*

The association of Persephone and Hades is probably a strand of the ancient veneration of the Mother as the bestower of all things and she to whom all departed when life had run its course. Not surprisingly this aspect of the Mother was rarely expressed but the Maiden and Mother partners were often to be seen in votive figures and works of art. This sixth-century terracotta shows them as identical. It comes from Corinth and is now in the British Museum.

*Plate 36*

Triptolemos was the son of the King of Eleusis who offered kindness to the exhausted Demeter after her wanderings. He alone recognized the goddess and it was he who told her that her daughter was in the possession of Hades. When Demeter was reunited with Persephone she rewarded Triptolemos with the knowledge of agriculture, and through him initiated the Mysteries at Eleusis. He was thereafter regarded as a culture hero; the spread of agriculture as the basis for an ordered and increasingly civilized life was attributed to him, and he was honoured at the Mysteries and at the Thesmophoria. He is seen here as a boy, receiving from Demeter the first sprig of corn. Bas-relief of the fifth century BC, now in the National Museum, Athens.

36

*Plate 37*

The ruins of the fifth-century temple of Demeter at Paestum. Paestum, which lies on the coast below Naples, was founded by Greek colonists in 600 BC. It flourished for centuries and was a wealthy city, as the impressive ruins testify; but the encroaching marshes made it unhealthy and it was gradually deserted during the Roman Empire.

37

39

## Plate 38

The Acropolis, seen from the Philopappus Hill. The word means 'upper city' and an eminence was commonly chosen in ancient times to give the city itself a citadel. The flat rock is 200 feet higher than Athens and, fittingly, it was the setting for the most famous temple ever built—the Parthenon, the temple of Athene Parthenos or Athene the Maiden. She was the patron goddess of Athens; the myth tells of the rivalry for the possession of Attica, and how Poseidon disputed Athene's claim. A council of the gods declared that the victor should be the one who gave to man the greatest gift. Poseidon struck the ground with his trident, and created the first horse. But Athene planted an olive tree and she was adjudged the victor. The meaning of the myth is plain: it is generally agreed by scholars that the figure of Athene goes back to archaic times, long before the Greeks arrived in the peninsula.

## Plate 39

Athene was the daughter of Zeus and Metis—an unwilling Metis who did her best to escape the god's attentions. Ge (Mother Earth) warned Zeus that the child of this union would be a girl but if he persisted in his attentions and she conceived a second child it would be a son, and depose him just as he had deposed his father Cronus. Zeus took no chances with any child of Metis: as soon as he could get close enough to her he swallowed her whole. In due course he began to feel violent headaches, which increased in severity so that his howling began to shake the heavens. Hermes divined the cause of discomfort; he fetched Hephaestos, who split Zeus' skull open. Athene sprang forth with a great shout, fully armed.

*Plate 40*

The Parthenon, constructed during the age of
Pericles between 447 and 438 BC. It was built
entirely of Pentelic marble and its perfect
proportions combine strength and grace; it is
the Doric style at the peak of perfection. The lovely
temple to Athene was revered for nearly a
thousand years; then the Byzantines gutted the
interior to make it a Christian church. This
barbarism was furthered by the Franks in
the thirteenth century AD, by the Turks in the
fifteenth, and by the Venetians in the seventeenth
century, so the Parthenon was a ruin when
Lord Elgin removed the sculptures in the nineteenth.
Many of them are in the British Museum.

*Plate 41*

Apollo, as the Etruscans saw him. A terracotta
statue of the fifth century BC from Veii depicts
a rather sinister god. Apollo was the son of
Zeus and Leto, daughter of the Titans
Coeus and Phoebe. Leto was the victim of
Hera's jealousy, and for fear of the goddess's
wrath no land would receive Leto when her time
drew near. She made her way to Ortygia near Delos;
the two islands floated in the sea, and only became
anchored after Leto's children were delivered. First
she gave birth to a girl, Artemis, who was no
sooner born than she helped her mother
cross to Delos. Apollo was born there on the
north side of Mount Cynthus and was a favoured
child from the beginning: Themis fed him on nectar
and ambrosia, and Hephaestos brought him arms
when he was only four days old. Apollo was a
late-comer among the gods of Greece, and probably
had his origins among the migrating peoples.
But the conception of a golden son, just and
beautiful and a benefactor, is a popular one and his
counterpart can be found in many mythologies.

42

43

Plate 42

Mount Parnassus in the spring, still crowned by
the winter snows. When he left Delos Apollo
went in search of the serpent Python, who
had at Hera's orders tormented Leto in her
wanderings. He found him on Parnassus and
wounded him with arrows; but Python managed
to escape and fled to the oracle of Mother Earth
at Delphi. Apollo dared to follow him into the
sacred place where he killed him by the chasm from
where the oracular utterances came.

Plate 43

Delphi lies on the south-west spur of Mount
Parnassus and was an oracular shrine in the time
before the Olympians, and the Greeks wisely chose
to maintain its reputation. When Apollo killed
Python there he was required to undergo
purification for defilining a holy place; but he
coaxed the art of prophecy from the god Pan
(significantly, Pan was a nature god as old as the
Mother herself) and then returned to Delphi.
He seized the shrine for himself and Delphi became
the most venerated site in Greece, the object of
endless pilgrimages where the priests of
Apollo sat on a tripod over the sacred
chasm giving the answers to the questions
of suppliants. The Delphic Oracle was the supreme
authority on matters of religion. Only two other
gods were represented at Delphi, Dionysus
and Athene. The picture shows the Tholos, one
of the buildings in the precinct dedicated to Athene.
It dates from the fourth century BC.

*Plate 44*

Apollo with his lyre, pouring a libation. He was the god of light (Phoebus, the bright), youth, prophecy and music—especially of the lyre. His other charge, the care of flocks and herds, points to his origin among the Indo-European migrants. Apollo's companions as the god of music—and of most the arts—were Dionysus as the patron of the theatre, and the Muses, the daughters of Zeus by Mnemosyne (memory). Apollo was a dangerous god to be involved with— King Midas was given asses' ears and Marsyas the satyr was flayed alive when they both doubted Apollo's musical supremacy—and it thus seems strange that the Greeks seemed to associate him with moral excellence. His cult in Delphi had an enormous influence in the extension of tolerance; it prescribed expiation for all crimes and actively discouraged the ancient idea of vengeance. But the Delphic Apollo is the later personification; the ancient god may well have been one to fear. The illustration is from a Greek dish of the fifth century BC, now in the museum at Delphi.

*44*

*Plate 45*

A relief of the first century BC showing a Muse playing a lyre. When the gods defeated the Titans Zeus was asked to create divinities capable of celebrating the victory. He lay with Mnmosyne for nine nights and the nine daughters of this union were the Muses. Though their preferred home was Mount Helicon they liked to visit Parnassus where they sought the waters of the Castalian spring and where they enjoyed the company of Apollo. The waters of the spring were used in purification rites in the temple at Delphi and were also given to the Pythoness (priestess) of the oracle to drink.

*45*

46

47

*Plate 46*

An early Greek terracotta, probably a votive offering, which represents the goddess Artemis. Homer describes Artemis as Mistress of Beasts and the description was as true of the goddess the Greeks venerated as it was of the Mother of whom she is another aspect. Like her twin brother Apollo she bore a name which was not Greek in origin but unlike him she was an original deity of Greece and the Aegean. Her origins, like those of so many Greek gods, clung to her even when she was transformed into an Olympian; thus she is a virgin goddess while at the same time a giver of fertility, and her domain is the wild earth, the forests and hills where she hunts. Again, her pleading with Asklepios to restore life to the dead Hippolytus suggests a very human and womanly love. In the tragedy by Euripides Hippolytus was presented as a man of perfect purity—a fit companion for Artemis. Possibly their story is a survival of the goddess's original character; as an aspect of the Mother she would have had a consort. The terracotta shown here portrays the Mistress of Beasts carrying a small unidentifiable animal, possibly a fawn. Small animals were sacrificed to her at her annual festival at Patrae.

*Plate 47*

Much more in keeping with the character of the Mother from whom she stemmed is the Artemis of Ephesus, the Ionian city which in classical times was a great seaport and the rival of Antioch and Alexandria. The cult of Artemis the giver of fertility had an ancient centre near the city and it was there that King Croesus ordered the building of a temple to her, a building which was to become one of the wonders of the ancient world. It was from Ephesus, not from Greece, that the cult of the goddess found its way to Rome. There, as Diana, she exacted the same confusion of venerations that she enjoyed in Greece. The city of Ephesus eventually declined; the silt of the Cayster river choked the harbour and now the remains of her glory lie several miles inland.

*Plate 48*

The virgin huntress. In this manifestation Artemis appears in the *Iliad*—and cuts rather a poor figure. She tries conclusions with the other Olympians present at the siege of Troy (the gods took definite sides in the struggle) and arouses the wrath of Hera, who tells her scornfully that the killing of animals is her proper place. However, if she *will* challenge her betters she must suffer the consequences: Hera then seizes Artemis' wrists in one hand and grabs her quiver and arrows with the other; she beats her victim about the head with them until the hapless Artemis breaks free and flies weeping to Olympus to be comforted by her father Zeus. Nevertheless Artemis was a firm favourite with women, especially those in the humbler walks of life who probably knew her best in her original form.

49

*Plate 49*

Hephaestos, the divine artificer and god of fire was the maker of magical things for gods and men, such as the armour of Achilles and Agamemnon's sceptre. The son of Zeus and Hera, he was such a sickly child at birth that Hera in disgust flung him from Olympus. He fell into the sea where Thetis (the mother of Achilles) and Eurynome found and cared for him, giving him a forge to work in. He made such exquisite jewellery that it attracted the attention of his cold-hearted mother and she had her son brought back to Olympus to take his proper place. Later he intervened in a quarrel between Hera and Zeus who hurled him from Olympus again. He returned to Olympus permanently lamed, but the strength of Hephaestos was in his mighty arms and shoulders which most metal workers develop. His cult centres were always to be found in the cities, where the craft was most intensely practised.

*Plate 50*

Boucher's painting *The Forges of Vulcan* is based on later accretions; the god is in fact Hephaestos and he is shown here with Aphrodite. The painting suggests domestic harmony; but the marriage was ordered by Zeus and Aphrodite resented being married off to the lame, ungainly smith god. Her lover was Ares, the war god, and the furious Hephaestos constructed an invisible net of bronze to cover the bed, and trapped the guilty pair by pretending to be absent. He then had his revenge when the rest of the Olympians gathered round to laugh at Ares and Aphrodite in their public humiliation.

50

*Plate 51*

The temple of Hephaestos in Athens, north-west of the Acropolis. Traditionally called the Theseum, this well-preserved small temple was mis-named, probably because some of the sculptures relate to the adventures of Theseus. It is now generally agreed that it was in fact a shrine to Hephaestos.

*51*

*Plate 52*

Aphrodite, the goddess of love. Homer and Hesiod differed in their account of her origins; Hesiod said that she arose from the sea foam which gathered around the genitals of Uranus when Cronus cast them down; Homer makes her the daughter of Zeus and Dione, and therefore a respectable member of the Olympian pantheon. She was in fact an ancient goddess of the eastern Mediterranean and can be equated with the Asian goddess Astarte. This marble statue from the Rhodes Museum shows her shaking out her hair after emerging from the waves. She was worshipped in Greece in two different manifestations, Aphrodite Urania (the higher, purer love) and Aphrodite Pandemos (sensual lust). Her worship was generally austere but it is interesting to note that prostitutes regarded her as their patron, and that there was a sacred prostitution in her cult at Corinth.

*52*

*Plate 53*

Dionysus returns to Greece to claim his place among the gods. To the north of Greece, in Thrace and Macedonia, there was in ancient times a powerful cult of the spirit of nature and fertility that expressed itself in orgiastic rites, human sacrifice and animal worship. This found its way to Greece around 1,000 BC and its ecstatic character made an irresistible appeal. At the centre of the cult was Dionysus, who came to represent the forces of life and nature in animals and the fruits of the growing plants; eventually he was regarded as the god of wine. But in earlier times there was no need for his followers— mostly women—to drink; their frenzies were self induced, and so uncontrollable that it was dangerous to encounter a band of women in a Dionysiac frenzy. Animals, and sometimes children, were torn to pieces and eaten—the belief existing that to devour a part of an animal was to partake of the god himself, a true sacramental meal.

*53*

54

55

*Plate 54*

An Etruscan terracotta showing the head of a satyr. The spirits of wild life, satyrs were bestial in both their desires and their behaviour and were often pictured with animal characteristics—those of a horse or a goat—to emphasize their connection with fertility. They were attendants on Dionysus, and some myths describe them as taking part in the tutoring of the young god.

*Plate 55*

An Etruscan bronze of the fifth century BC showing a satyr and a maenad. The maenads were votaries of Dionysus—the word means 'mad women', a description of their behaviour during their frenzied worship. In the play by Euripides, *The Bacchae*, the cult of Dionysus is resisted by Pentheus, King of Thebes, and his mother Agave. Dionysus rouses the women of Thebes to a frenzy and sends them to take part in his rites on the mountainside; then the god reappears in the guise of a votary and persuades the king to spy on them, inducing the same frenzy in Agave that affects the other women. The hapless Pentheus is torn to pieces by the maenads, and Agave returns to the palace carrying a head she has torn from a man's shoulders. Only when her frenzy abates does she realize that the head is her son's. Followers of the god were also called *bakchoi*, and the name Bacchus was the Latin one used by the Romans for their version of Dionysus.

*Plate 56*

The theatre at Delphi. Dionysus was made respectable by Hesiod, and joined the Olympians as the son of Zeus and Semele. Apollo is credited with the 'taming' of the wilder excesses of Dionysiac religion. During the older, more bestial orgies the maenads often wore masks, and the god was represented by a mask on a pole; the pole was draped with an animal skin but the mask was always human, and this aspect of the cult was the beginning of drama as an art. Apollo admitted Dionysus to his side at Delphi—in other words the powerful cult was admitted to the gentler forms of state religion. By the fifth century BC dramatic festivals were an integral part of Greek culture; one of the most noteworthy festivals was the great Dionysia—the spring festival of Dionysus.

*Plate 57*

Hermes with the infant Dionysus. Hermes was given his place on Olympus by Homer, who made him the son of Zeus and Maia, the daughter of Atlas. In fact he was one of the oldest of the original Greek gods; he was the god of luck and wealth and dreams; patron of merchants—and of thieves; god of the roads and, in Arcadia, of fertility. These ancient attributes were easily metamorphosed when he took his place on Olympus and his most frequent appearance is as a messenger or guide. Here he is seen taking the infant Dionysus to Nysa to entrust him to the care of the nymphs. This famous statue was found in the ruins of the temple of Hera at Olympia and was at first believed to be an original of Praxiteles, *c* 330 BC. It is now generally agreed that the statue is a later copy.

*Plate 58*

Three Olympians on a Greek amphora. To the left is Hermes wearing his winged sandals, and Dionysus is on the right, crowned with vine leaves and negligently spilling wine from a vessel in his right hand. The goddess in the centre is the virgin of the hearth, Hestia described by Hesiod as the daughter of Cronus and Rhea and thus the sister of Zeus. The hearth fire was the most important thing in the life of early settled man; without it he had no protection or warmth. Obviously it was a sacred principle and the goddess who personified it remained little more than that —there are no myths surrounding her after her establishment on Olympus. She took part in no wars or disputes, and was generally regarded as the most gentle of the family of gods.

57

# IV
# OTHER GODS, SPIRITS OF LAND AND SEA

59

*Plate 59*

The setting sun burnishes the ruins of a classical temple on the island of Rhodes. According to legend the island was the domain of the sun god, Helios; he was able to discern its coming from the sea and he claimed it before the other gods knew of its existence. Rhodos, the nymph of the island (in some traditions the daughter of Aphrodite) became the sun god's consort and she bore him seven sons. The island held an annual festival in honour of Helios and a great festival every fourth year.

60

61

62

*Plate 60*

The sun god depicted on a Greek krater. A team of four winged horses drew his chariot across the sky; when it had crossed the heavens it sank into the western sea, and rose again in the east to bring the returning day. (During the annual festival on Rhodes a team of four horses was sacrificed by being thrown into the sea). Helios was later confused with Apollo—probably because of Apollo's other name which was Phoebus (the bright). But Helios was the original sun god of the Greeks, identified by them as the spirit of a natural phenomenon. For that reason he enjoyed no particular veneration and there was no cult of Helios on the Greek mainland. However he was acknowledged as one who saw and heard everything, and in the *Iliad* Agamamnon calls upon him to witness the oath he takes before the duel of Paris and Menelaus.

*Plate 61*

Selene, the goddess of the moon. Like Helios, she was to be confused in later legends with other deities. Some traditions described her as the sister of the sun god, and appropriately she was most often confused with Artemis the sister of Apollo. Unlike Helios, she had no cult of her own, though evidence suggests that there was something like a moon cult in Crete in very early times. Despite this the Greeks shared with their contemporaries the superstitions about the moon and its influence on organic and erotic life; everything prospered and increased when the moon waxed—the opposite happened when the moon waned. Magic was practised in the light of the rising moon, and the full moon was the time when physical passion would be most intense. The illustration shown here is a detail from a Greek krater and shows Selene on her horse. The moon is in the descendent and goddess and mount are beginning to sink from sight.

*Plate 62*

Asklepios, the god of healing and medicine. That is according to Hesiod—to Homer he was a mortal who was taught the art of healing by Chiron the centaur. Hesiod made him the son of Apollo by the nymph, Coronis, who proved faithless to her divine lover; he complained to his sister Artemis, who killed the nymph with arrows. Then, while watching her funeral pyre burn, Apollo was filled with remorse and he snatched the unborn child of Coronis from the flames. The child was Asklepios and Apollo entrusted him to the care of Chiron. The versions of Homer and Hesiod agree at least on the point that it was from Chiron that he learned the art of healing. Asklepios sometimes incurred the wrath of Zeus and his brother Hades; his skill as a healer could deprive Zeus of revenge by bringing his victim back to life, and deprive Hades' kingdom of inhabitants simply by ensuring that they did not die. He is shown here with his staff and his serpent emblem which signified renewal.

63

*Plate 63*

The theatre at Epidauros, the Greek city which
owed its fame to Asklepios—the centre of his cult
was here. Patients would visit the temple and sleep
there; a cure would sometimes be communicated
through dreams, sometimes be effected during
sleep. Snakes were kept in the temple and
regarded as sacred, the snake being the
god's emblem, and when new cult centres
were founded young serpents were taken there
from Epidauros. (The small yellow snakes to be seen
in the region today, harmless creatures, are very
likely those described by the ancient Greek
traveller Pausanias). The theatre dates from the
fourth century BC and is one of the most perfect of
its kind. It is in regular use today.

64

65

66

*Plate 64*

The great god Pan depicted in bronze by an Etruscan sculptor of the fourth century BC. A very ancient god indeed, his cult was in Arcadia where Mount Maenalus was sacred to him. A herdsman's god, he came to be associated with goats which were the principal livestock of that part of Greece. In Homer he is made the son of Hermes who was an Olympian and also, originally, a god of Arcadia. The cult of Pan reached beyond his native pastures and by the fifth century BC he had a cave shrine on the Acropolis. He was reputed to be the cause of sudden and groundless fear—panic fear—that could overcome people in desolate, lonely places, and his principal diversion, sex, was the natural outcome of his connection with the fertility of flocks. Though a minor god in classical Greece, Pan enjoyed a healthy respect. It was from him that Apollo learned the art of prophecy.

*Plate 65*

An Etruscan terracotta relief from Cerveteri showing a satyr dancing with a maenad. Satyrs were originally shown with some animal-like features, those of a horse or a goat, and were variously called the brothers of the nymphs or the spirits of the wild countryside. They were associated with both Dionysus and Pan and in later Greek art often depicted as the familiars of Dionysus in his character of god of wine. As the familiars of Pan they often wore horns and walked on hoofs and this association, particularly, was the one that gave them in later centuries their identification as the male symbols of sexuality. The satyr shown here seems little more than a frisky young man; but in Roman art that is how he frequently appears.

*Plate 66*

A Lycian sarcophagus of the fourth century BC, showing two centaurs in combat on the front panel. These strange creatures were originally depicted as horses with the head of a man. The later, more familiar idea of a creature half man and half horse is seen here. They are very old in Greek legend, much older than Homer and they appear in both of his epics. In mythology, the centaurs were begotten by Ixion, who abused the hospitality of Zeus by casting lustful eyes on Hera. Zeus divined his intentions and fashioned a false Hera from a cloud. Ixion, too drunk to notice anything wrong, seduced the cloud woman, Nephele, and was then bound by Zeus in punishment to a fiery wheel which rolled across the sky eternally, while Nephele descended to earth and gave birth to a son, Centaurus. This son mated with the mares of Mount Pelion and thus sired the race of centaurs. Generally they were wild, lustful, and strongly attracted to wine. The exception was the wise and kind medicine-man Chiron, who differed from the others being of divine origin.

*Plate 67 and 68*

Eros was the god of love in Greek mythology, the son of Aphrodite by either Ares or Hermes (there are differing traditions). Homer never mentions Eros as a god, simply referring to *eros* as the force that impels lovers to one another—and makes wise men speak in the language of fools. Hesiod on the other hand believed him to be one of the oldest and most powerful gods, since neither men nor the gods themselves were proof against him. As the personification of physical love he had a large following among the Greeks and he was celebrated annually in a number of festivals. The one in Athens was held in the Spring and phallic symbols have been found in the ruins of his sanctuary. In Greek art he was originally shown as a young man carrying his bow and walking over flowers and plants, as in the gold-painted lekythos. By the Hellenistic period he had become the more familiar baby-like figure, often asleep, as in the marble statue from Paphos.

67

68

69

70

*Plate 69*

Chiron the centaur with the young Achilles. Chiron played the part of mentor and guardian to Achilles, Jason, Heracles and many other Greek heroes. He was possibly in origin a priest-king of the horse breeders of Thessaly, one to whom they ascribed all wisdom. It was inevitable that his stature increased as the tradition extended down the centuries. Some myths describe him as the king of the centaurs; others say that he was the son of Cronus and therefore immortal. His immortality was to prove no boon; Heracles, while performing his Fourth Labour, accidentally wounded Chiron in the knee—and Heracles used arrows dipped in the poison of Hydra. The wound would have been fatal to a mortal but for Chiron it was infinitely worse, since he would have to endure eternal pain. At length the cruel impasse was overcome; Zeus allowed Chiron to surrender his immortality to Prometheus, and die in peace. Wall painting from Herculaneum.

*Plate 70*

A view of the Greek countryside with a glimpse of Delphi in the distance. The Greeks acknowledged the spirits of nature in many different ways and the most familiar to us are perhaps the nymphs. Usually believed to be young and beautiful, they were benevolent to mankind as a rule but were not to be trifled with. They punished unresponsive lovers and sometimes stole young men for themselves; they were very like the fairies of later days. There was an infinite variety of them; those of the forests and groves were Dryads, those of meadows Leimoniads, those of mountains Orestiads. There were also the water nymphs; Naiads, Potameids, Creneids and Hydriads. In contrast to the gods the nymphs were mortal, though they were blessed, according to Hesiod, with very long lives.

*Plate 71*

A Harpy carrying off a child. The Harpies (the name is from a Greek word meaning 'snatchers') were, according to Homer and Hesiod, the personification of violent winds—strong enough to snatch people away. They were usually depicted as birds with the faces of women, and in mythology they are described as the daughters of Thaumas and Electra (daughter of Oceanus—not the sister of Orestes). They make a notable appearance in the story of the Argonauts: when the voyagers reached Salmydessus they found the king, Phineus, in great distress because the Harpies continually plagued him. He had the gift of prophecy, and had earned the wrath of Zeus for using his gift too accurately. The Harpies snatched the food from his table and defiled what they couldn't carry away. The Argonauts rid Phineus of the Harpies, and in turn he gave them valuable advice about the voyage. The relief shown here is in the British Museum and comes from a tomb of the fifth century BC found at Xanthos in Asia Minor.

# V
# THE STUFF OF TRAGEDY

72

*Plate 72*

Orpheus and the beasts as depicted on a mosaic from Tarsus of the third
century AD. Orpheus is one of the most celebrated figures in Greek mythology—
and one of the most difficult to identify. According to the myths surrounding
him he was the son of the Muse Calliope, and a musician of such power and
sweetness that the wild creatures would gather to listen to him. He sailed with the
Argonauts, and his wife was the dryad Eurydice who, fleeing from the
attentions of Aristaeus, trod on a serpent and died from its bite. Orpheus went
down to Hades and persuaded him to release her; but the lord of the shades
made the condition that Orpheus must believe that Eurydice followed him to
earth—and not look back. But in his agony of uncertainty that Eurydice
was really following him Orpheus did look back, and saw her slip away from him
for ever.

*Plate 73*

The Lion Gate, the entrance to the citadel of
Mycenae. Agamemnon was king of Mycenae and
the leader of the Achaean armies that went to Troy
to avenge the stealing of Helen, the most beautiful
of all women and the wife of Menelaus, the king of
Sparta. The brothers and their Achaean allies
were eventually victorious—but the war had
dragged on for ten years. Agamemnon,
who may well have been an historic personage,
might have ridden under the Lion Gate in
the chariot that brought him home, apparently
in triumph. Also in the chariot would have been
Cassandra, the princess of Troy he claimed as part of
his spoils. But there had been another princess—
Agamemnon's daughter Iphigenia, and he had
used her as a sacrifice when the Achaen fleet was
held up at Aulis by contrary winds. He tricked his
wife Clytemnestra into bringing the girl to
Aulis, saying that she was to become the
wife of Achilles. Clytemnestra had been waiting ten
years for the king to return. . . .

73

*Plate 74*

. . . and in her husband's absence she took a lover,
Aegisthus, and waited for the day when she could be
revenged on Agamemnon. When he returned
from Troy she gave him a welcome befitting a
warrior king; but then murdered both him
and Cassandra when they entered the palace.
This is one of the strange beehive tombs of Mycenae,
which were built into the side of the hill and given
their shape by the use of the corbeled vault. This
is variously called 'the Treasury of Atreus' and
'the Tomb of Clytemnestra' but the actual
use to which the building was put cannot
be determined. If it was indeed a tomb for
Clytemnestra its strangeness is well suited to
the extraordinary woman the Greek tragedians
put into their plays. She is a tremendous figure in
the *Agamemnon* of Aeschylus; and also appears in the
sequel, *The Liberation Bearers*.

74

*Plate 75*

A fifth-century terracotta showing Electra and
Orestes at the tomb of Agamemnon. The
great tragic cycle which begins with the
sacrifice of Iphigenia rolls on relentlessly. The
most famous dramatic version of the next stage of
events is probably the *Electra* of Sophocles but
the scene shown here, moving though it is, is not
used by that master. It occurs in the *Electra* of
Euripides and *The Libation Bearers* of Aeschylus, and
deals with the encounter of brother and sister at
their father's tomb. In the play by Aeschylus,
Orestes has been in exile since the murder of his
father. He returns with his friend Pylades
and, going at once to his father's tomb,
dedicates on it a lock of his hair. The two
withdraw upon the approach of Electra and her
attendants, who have been sent to pour libations on
the tomb by their guilty mother Clytemnestra
who has been troubled by ominous dreams. Electra
recognizes the lock of hair—exactly like her own
—and brother and sister are reunited.

75

76

77

*Plate 76*

Orestes avenges the death of his father, Agamemnon. Detail from an amphora in the British Museum. After the encounter at the tomb, Orestes and Pylades proceed to the palace in disguise and tell Clytemnestra that Orestes her son is dead. Exultant, the queen sends for her lover Aegisthus, believing that there can be no threat now to their happiness and safety. When Aegisthus arrives Orestes kills him in front of the Queen. She pleads for her life, and Orestes falters; but he has been commanded by Apollo and drags his mother inside the palace and murders her too.

*Plate 77*

Cadmus, the brother of Europa and the founder of Thebes. The Delphic oracle told him to follow a cow and found a city where the creature first lay down. This he did, then Athene instructed him to sow the teeth of the dragon he had just killed, and from them grew warriors fully armed. Cadmus provoked these to fight each other by throwing a stone amongst them, and the five best fighters who survived became the ancestors of the noble families of Thebes.

*Plate 78*

The meeting with the Sphinx, an incident in the tragic life of Oedipus, who became king of Thebes. His father Laius had brought a curse on his family and he was warned by Apollo that his own son would kill him. This was Oedipus, and Laius drove a spike through the baby's feet and left him to die on Mount Cithaeron. A shepherd found him and took him to Polybus and Merope, king and queen of Corinth, who brought him up as their son. Later, upset by taunts that he was no true son of Polybus, Oedipus enquired of the Delphic oracle concerning his true parentage. The oracle only told him that he would bring destruction on his father and marry his own mother, and the horrified Oedipus, loving Polybus and Merope as the only parents he knew, fled from Corinth to avoid doing them harm. On his journey he came to a place where three roads met, and there encountered a man in a chariot who ordered him to get out of his way. A fight ensued and Oedipus killed the man in the chariot who was Laius, his real father. Oedipus went on, and defeated the Sphinx that plagued the city of Thebes, and as a result he was welcomed as a hero. He was offered the hand of Jocasta, the widowed queen, and the throne—the oracle was fulfilled. By his wife-mother, Oedipus became the father of two sons and two daughters, and all went well until, in a time of famine and disease, the oracle was to wreak havoc with him again; the city would know peace, it said, when the unknown murderer of Laius was discovered and cast out. Oedipus sets out to find the truth, and when he does it is too awful to bear; Jocasta hangs herself and Oedipus puts out his eyes. He leaves the city, a blinded exile, attended by his daughter Antigone.

# VI
# THE HEROES

79

*Plate 79*

Heracles was the hero of heroes. No one else has left such an impression of
undefeatable strength and fearlessness and it is possible that the character
was based on an ancient hero of Argos who actually lived. His character suggests
that he was much older than the others, like Theseus and Jason; his adventures
depend entirely on his brute strength while the other heroes display a certain wit
and intelligence in the performance of their exploits. Heracles was inclined to
force even when dealing with the gods, as this incident shows. He had
gone to Delphi seeking to be rid of evil dreams after his murder of Iphitus;
the Pythoness had refused to counsel such as he, whereupon he seized the tripod
and smashed the votive offerings in the shrine. When Apollo, wrathful at
such desecration, appeared on the scene Heracles fought him and they
were eventually separated by their father Zeus. The Greeks usually depicted
Heracles as a trim, often handsome man, in contrast to the muscle-bound
heavyweight the Romans made of him.

*Plate 80*

Heracles was the son of Zeus, who lay with
Alcmena in the guise of her absent husband
Amphitryon, making the night last three
times as long to ensure his begetting. Hera,
jealous again at Zeus' coupling with a mortal
woman, afflicted Heracles with madness, and the
famous Labours were a penalty for the crimes
committed during this time. He had to serve
Eurystheus, king of Tiryns, for twelve years and
perform whatever Labours the king imposed. The
First Labour is shown on this Attic vase painting,
where Heracles kills the lion that was ravaging
Nemea. He skinned the lion with its own
claws and thereafter wore the pelt as a cloak.

*Plate 81*

Heracles and the Hind of Ceryneia. Another one of
his Labours was the catching of this creature, a
dappled deer with hooves of brass and golden
horns (the horns suggest that it may in fact
have been a stag) sacred to the goddess
Artemis. Four such hinds were harnessed
to the chariot of Artemis; the fifth was the
one Heracles pursued, the last of the original herd.
He hunted her for one whole year and ran her
down, exhausted, near the river Ladon. This detail
from an Attic vase painting shows Heracles
wearing his lion-skin cloak. He is watched by
Athene and Artemis, the latter on the right carrying
her huntress's bow.

80

81

82

*Plate 82*

Tiryns, the city most associated with the
myths of Heracles, was a very ancient one and
possibly existed as long ago as 2,500 BC. The ruins
can be seen in the plain of Argos, to the south
of Mycenae, and their most famous feature is the
incredible walls built of huge roughly-hewn blocks
which in some places are more than twenty-five
feet thick. Like nearby Mycenae, Tiryns stood on a
hill and was a strong fortress; it survived as an
inhabited city until it was destroyed by the
city of Argos in the early fourth century BC.

83

*Plate 83*

Heracles carries the Erymanthian boar back alive.
A bronze figure now in the Delphi museum. It
was while engaged on this Labour that
Heracles accidentally wounded Chiron the
centaur. On his way to Mount Erymanthus he
was entertained by the centaur Pholus, who
possessed a jar of wine given him by Dionysus.
When the jar was opened the other centaurs smelled
the wine and attacked the cave where Pholus and
Heracles were enjoying a meal. Chiron, hearing the
noise of the fight, went to see what the trouble
was and it was then that an arrow of Heracles'
wounded him in the knee.
Heracles eventually caught the boar. It was hidden
in a thicket and he shouted until it emerged; then
he drove it up the hillside toward a deep
snowdrift. The speed of the beast was
thus reduced and he was able to catch up
with it. He bound it with chains and carried it
on his shoulders to king Eurystheus, who was
so terrified by the struggling, snarling creature that
he jumped into a bronze jar to hide from it.

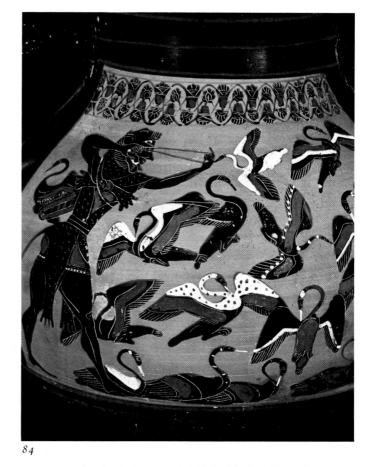

Plate 84

The Stymphalian birds were sacred to Ares. They were man-eaters and had claws and wings of brass and their excrement was poisonous to the crops. They lived in the Stymphalian marsh and the people of the neighbouring countryside went in terror of them; sometimes in flight they would shed their brazen feathers from a great height which were as dangerous as arrows. Heracles paused by the marsh and could devise no way of dealing with the plague; he could not walk in the soft mud and he could not use a boat among the thick reeds. The goddess Athene came to his aid in this Labour; on her advice he took a brass rattle and climbed on to a spur of Mount Cyllene. He made a mighty noise, and continued with such persistence that the birds took fright and flew up from the marsh. He was then able to kill many of them with arrows. He repeated this trick and so decimated the flock that the remainder, terrified, flew off to the east and left the region in peace. Detail from a fifth-century amphora.

84

Plate 85

As a penalty for desecrating the shrine at Delphi, Heracles had to serve as a slave for one year. His owner was Omphale, the queen of Lydia, and one of the services he performed for her was the capture of two clever thieves, the Cercopes. He tied their feet and hung them head downward from a pole; then he swung them across his shoulders and carried them off to justice. He had gone a little way when he noticed that his captives were whispering to each other— soon they were chuckling. Their laughter continued and by paying attention to their whispers Heracles realized that they were laughing at him. He wore only his lion-skin cloak, which reached no farther down than his waist; his buttocks and thighs were constantly exposed to the sun. The Cercopes were exchanging wisecracks about 'old black-bottom' their captor. In the end he started laughing himself, and was persuaded to let them go. A relief of the sixth century BC from Selinunte.

85

86

87

*Plate 86*

Heracles and the centaur Nessus. The hero won the hand of Deianira, princess of Calydon, and on the way to Trachis they found the river Euenus in flood. Heracles could not breast the flood and carry Deianira as well, so he agreed that the centaur Nessus should ferry the princess across. No sooner was Deianira mounted on the centaur's back than Nessus galloped away with her. An arrow from Heracles stopped his flight, and while he lay dying Nessus told Deianira to keep some of his blood, and smear it on her husband's clothes to prevent him being unfaithful to her; and this Deianira did. She remembered the centaur's advice when Heracles announced his intention of marrying another woman, and sent him a robe anointed with the blood of Nessus. It was fatal; the arrows of Heracles were poisoned with the blood of the Hydra—Nessus knew that perfectly well and his blood was poisoned too. Heracles, to end his agony, had a funeral pyre prepared. He was carried to it, and upon his death took his place with his father Zeus on Olympus.

*Plate 87*

One adventure of Heracles was oddly confused with those of another hero, Theseus, and it is generally believed that some of the former's deeds were unsuccessfully grafted on to those of the latter to increase his heroic status. In this fragment from Delphi Theseus is shown defeating the Amazon queen; the Amazons had invaded Attica when Theseus abducted one of them, Antiope. Heracles, in his adventure, was to capture the girdle of Hippolyta, queen of the Amazons, because the daughter of Eurystheus wanted it. He succeeded in getting it, and there are various accounts of how this was done. One version says that he killed her for it; but the Amazon wife of Theseus was called Hippolyta—she might have been another Amazon queen but the appearance of her name in both adventures suggests that one adventure has not very successfully been made into two.

*Plate 88*

Heracles about to embark on another adventure, and one in which he played a minor part. This painting on a fifth-century krater shows the Argonauts gathering for their voyage, under the command of Jason, to capture the Golden Fleece. Jason was the son of Aeson, king of Iolcos. Aeson's kingdom was usurped by his half-brother Pelias, and Jason was sent for safety to the care of Chiron the centaur. As a man he returned to Pelias' court; the king sent him on the quest for the Golden Fleece, hoping to be rid of the threat to his uneasy throne. Jason built the *Argo* and fifty Greek heroes, including Heracles and Orpheus, sailed with him to Colchis at the eastern shore of the Black Sea. The goddess Athene is standing on the left, while Jason converses with Heracles who is as usual naked except for his lion skin. Jason succeeded in his quest, largely because of the help given him by the witch-queen of Colchis, Medea, who fell in love with him.

89

*Plate 89*

The interior of a painted kylix from Vulci showing the exploits of Theseus. The centre is occupied by the most famous exploit of all—the encounter with the Minotaur; directly above it he can be seen wrestling with Kerkyon, who waylaid travellers near Eleusis and challenged them to wrestle with him. Through his brute strength he usually won; but Theseus brought skill to the combat and managed to kill him. Reading clockwise, the next scene shows him killing Procrustes, who had a nasty habit of trimming—or stretching—his guests to fit his bed. Next is the evil Sinis, whose victims were hurled to their death on trees which he bent down to the ground for the purpose. Third is the great bull that ravaged the plain of Marathon, and then Sciron the bandit who threw his victims into the sea. The pictures end with Theseus defeating the monstrous sow bred by Phaea of Crommyon, which so terrorised the people that they dared not venture into their fields. At length Theseus reached Athens, only to meet another, more subtle, danger. His father Aegeus had in the meantime married the witch-queen Medea, whom Jason had brought back from Colchis and then spurned. She nearly succeeded in poisoning Theseus; but Aegeus recognized the sword that Theseus carried and dashed the cup from his hand. So Theseus took his rightful place in Athens, and it wasn't long before he set out on the greatest adventure of all.

*Plate 90*

Theseus was a hero of Athens, and that city claimed him as the true founder of the state. One of the early kings, Aegeus, stopped at the city of Troezen on his way back from Delphi, and made love to the princess Aethra. (Some versions have it that she was also loved by Poseidon, and that Theseus was in fact the son of a god. He enjoyed the sea-god's protection during his adventures.) When Aegeus returned to Athens, he left his sword and his sandals concealed under a heavy rock; he told Aethra that if she bore a son, and he could succeed in lifting the rock and recover the tokens—then Aegeus would acknowledge him as his heir. Theseus was only sixteen when he succeeded in this task; he could have sailed to Athens there and then but he preferred to go by land, crossing the dangerous Isthmus road. That was the beginning of his exploits. This Roman relief of the late first century AD shows him lifting the rock—and looking rather more than sixteen years old. The relief is now in the British Museum.

90

*Plate 91*

An Attic amphora of the fifth century BC, showing the killing of the Minotaur in realistic detail. King Aegeus was obliged to send seven youths and seven maidens each year to Crete, a penalty for the death, in Athens, of Androgeos the son of the Cretan king, Minos. None of them ever returned; upon reaching his kingdom Minos put them in the Labyrinth—a maze from which it was impossible to escape—to be devoured by the Minotaur. The Minotaur was the offspring of the queen, Pasiphae, who conceived an unnatural passion for a fine bull that emerged from the sea. The result of this union was a creature half man and half bull, and the Labyrinth was constructed by Daedalus to hide it in.

Theseus volunteered to go as one of the seven youths. When the ship arrived in Crete the king's daughter Ariadne saw him and fell in love with him, and it was she who conceived the idea of using a ball of thread, given her by Daedalus, to show Theseus the way in and out of the Labyrinth. The ball of thread unwound itself, showing him the way to the Minotaur's lair. He killed the monster, and then followed the thread to escape from the maze. He and his companions fled from Crete, taking Ariadne with them, and stopped at Naxos on the way home. Some traditions say that while on Naxos the hero was visited by Dionysus in a dream; the god demanded Ariadne for himself. Whatever the reason for it, Theseus did abandon Ariadne, who lay weeping on the shore until Dionysus, returning to Greece, reached the island and consoled her with his love.

91

*Plate 92*

Perseus slaying the Gorgon. A sixth-century relief from Selinunte. This hero was, like Heracles, a son of Zeus; his mother was Danae, daughter of Acrisius who really wanted a son. The oracle told him that he would have no heir—but to beware of his daughter's son. He promptly imprisoned her in an underground chamber; but it was too late —she had been seen by Zeus and the god visited her as a shower of gold which poured into her lap. Danae seems to have had a fatal fascination; her father cast her adrift in a chest on the sea as soon as her son was born, and it drifted to the island of Seriphus. The king of Seriphus immediately fell in love with her, and decided to get rid of her son. Perseus was sent to get the Gorgon's head, and a glance from the Gorgon could turn any man to stone. However he was fortunate in his allies: with winged sandals from Hermes he could fly, with a cap from Hades he could become invisible, and in some versions Athene leant him her shield to use as a mirror and thus avoid the Gorgon's glance. Athene is seen here beside the hero, and in the Gorgon's lap is Pegasus. (The magic horse was the child of the Gorgon by Poseidon, and in this relief is, strangely, shown without the wings which were his most famous feature).

92

# VII
# ILIAD & ODYSSEY

93

*Plate 93*

It is not known for certain when it was that Homer wrote, though the scant evidence that exists suggests that it was some time in the eighth century BC. His life is also unknown to us; the few hints that can be gleaned from the text of the *Iliad* have led to the assumption that he was a Greek of Ionia but there is nothing positive. This has led to doubt that there ever was a tragic poet who composed two great epics, that what we know as the *Iliad* and the *Odyssey* were simply collections of heroic lays strung together over a period of time. Most scholars now dismiss that theory; the poems bear the evidence of a single creator in their unity of style and their consistency of character. They could not have simply evolved.

The *Iliad* concerns the war between Troy and the Achaens (Homer never calls them Greeks) over the abduction of Helen by the Trojan prince, Paris. The *Odyssey* is the long, adventurous journey home of the king of Ithaca, Odysseus, who went to the war unwillingly but proved as valint as—and much cleverer than—Achilles, Ajax, Diomedes, Menelaus, Agememnon and the rest. The illustration, from a Lucanian krater, shows Odysseus and Diomedes in one of the lesser known incidents; they make a raid by night on the Trojan lines and stumble on Dolon, a Trojan who was attempting to spy on the Achaean camp. Dolon proves unequal to the ordeal of their threats and gives them valuable information. But they murder him anyway.

*Plate 94*

Menelaus and Hector, the Trojan prince, in combat. The dead man is the Trojan, Euphorbus, and this painted plate from Rhodes is known as the Euphorbus plate. Patroclus led the attack on Troy while Achilles was sulking in his tent, and Euphorbus gave him his first wound; Hector finished him off. Menelaus killed Euphorbus—but did not long try conclusions with the great Hector. However, he and Ajax returned for the body of Patroclus and bore it back to the Achaean camp. It was this that roused Achilles from his sulks; he loved Patroclus, and the news that he was killed roused Achilles to fury. He meant to have Hector's life in return.

*Plate 95*

Hector and Achilles face to face. Achilles mounted a furious attack on the Trojans that drove them back into the city. Hector met him at the Scaean Gate and the two champions knew that one of them must fall. It was Hector. To the horror of the Trojans watching from the walls, Achilles despoiled the corpse by tying it to the back of his chariot and dragging it through the dust back to his camp. There he sacrificed twelve Trojan prisoners on the funeral pyre of Patroclus; but he intended that Hector's body should be thrown to the dogs. In the meantime he went on despoiling it, but Apollo was moved to compassion and preserved his body from damage. On the twelfth day the gods, outraged by Achilles' vile behaviour, decided that Hector's body should be restored to his father Priam for decent burial. The Messenger goddess Iris went to Troy, and inspired Priam to go to the Achaen camp. The old king pleaded with Achilles, and finally yielded his daughter Polyxena as a bride for Achilles as well as Hector's weight in gold. Achilles gave way, and the corpse of the noble Hector was taken back to Troy for burial.

94

96

97

*Plate 96*

After the wooden Horse. The Achaeans took the city, and no mercy was shown to the Trojans. Cassandra, Priam's daughter, fled to the temple of Athene for sanctuary. She was pursued there by Ajax who dragged her away from the altar; thus he earned the wrath of Athene and the loathing of the other Achaeans for violating a sacred shrine. The painting of this fourth-century lekythos shows Apollo watching the scene. Apollo had fallen in love with Cassandra but she had resisted him; in consequence the god had given her the gift of prophecy—and then made it useless. No one believed her, though she had in fact prophesied the city's doom. Ajax had to yield Cassandra to Agamemnon when the spoils were divided, and she met the same fate as her captor when he returned to Mycenae.

*Plate 97*

The sack of Troy. Priam, lying on the ground, was killed by Neoptolemus, the son of Achilles. Hecuba, the queen of Troy, fell to the lot of Odysseus, though this fact was lost in the telling of his subsequent adventures. The son of Hector and Andromache, the last of the Trojan royal line, is seen being carried off by the Achaean herald, Talthybius. The child could not be allowed to live, and Talthybius, acting on the orders of Odysseus, hurled him from the walls. Andromache was given to Neoptolemus, and Polyxena was sacrificed on the tomb of Achilles. The beautiful Helen, the apparent cause of the war, was threatened with death by her husband Menelaus but her beauty destroyed his resolve and he took her back to Sparta with him. The Achaeans destroyed the city by fire after plundering it.

*Plate 98*

On his way home from Troy Odysseus landed on the island of the Cyclops, giant herdsmen who were said to be the sons of Poseidon, and who had only one eye. Odysseus and his companions explored a cave which proved to be the home of one of the Cyclops, Polyphemus, who returned unexpectedly and sealed the exit with a huge rock after his flock of sheep were safely inside. He discovered the men and promptly ate two of them; the next day he ate two more. Odysseus, in the way of epic heroes, just happened to have a full wine-skin with him, which sent Polyphemus into a drunken sleep. Odysseus took a burning brand from the fire in the cave and thrust it into the giant's single eye; Polyphemus in his agony screamed for his brother Cyclops to come and help him. Now Odysseus, asked by Polyphemus who he was, had answered 'I am Noman'. When his brother Cyclops asked Polyphemus what he was screaming about he told them that Noman had blinded him. They went away again, annoyed that he should be raving about something that no man was doing to him; and assuming he was having nightmares.

*Plate 99*

Odysseus and Circe, from a Theban vase of the fourth century. Circe, looking somewhat less than an enchantress, offers a drink to Odysseus, who looks somewhat less than a hero. The events of the Trojan war and the return of Odysseus were favourite subjects among the Greek painters and the quality of the work was, inevitably, of enormous range, and this representation is not one of the best. On the island of Aeaea Odysseus went off to explore, and when he returned to the ship divided his company into two parties to go and investigate the smoke he had seen rising from a clearing. One party found the palace of Circe; she invited them in and gave them food and drink. But the food turned them into pigs. Odysseus, going to their rescue, was warned by the god Hermes, who gave him a magic herb known only to the gods. So Odysseus was immune to Circe's magic, and he forced her to restore his men to their human form. However he was not immune to Circe's personal charms; he dallied with her for a whole year.

99

*Plate 100*

When Odysseus finally reached Ithaca he disguised himself as a beggar on the advice of the goddess Athene. His first encounter was with his old swineherd Eumaeus, who told the stranger of what had befallen in the palace while the king was away on a war from which he had never returned; that the palace was full of suitors despoiling the king's household, and trying to persuade Penelope, the queen, to marry one of them in the hope of gaining the throne. Odysseus continued to the palace, having made himself known to his son Telemachus, and there was only recognized by his old dog Argus who, lying neglected on a dung heap, was able to give him one last, hopeful wag of his tail before dying. Penelope, hearing from the stranger that he knew her husband, treated him as an honoured guest and asked his old nurse, Eurycleia, to bring water and wash the stranger's feet. The incident is shown here on a Roman relief of the first century AD. Eurycleia recognized Odysseus by an old scar from a wound he had sustained while hunting boar. Eventually Odysseus made himself known to Penelope; but not until he had killed the suitors and regained his kingdom.

100

# Roman Mythology

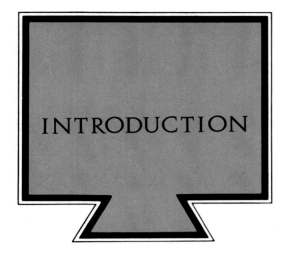

# INTRODUCTION

'Ancient Rome' — to us the two words are almost synonymous. When we think of antiquity, it is to Rome that our thoughts automatically turn; and the mere sound of the word Rome is to our ears like the echo of some melancholy passing-bell, tolling for the demise of a glory that is no more.

But the Romans did not think in those terms at all. For them, Rome was forever young and sprightly, 'eternal' in fact, an epithet the Romans themselves applied to their city as early as the latter days of the Republic. They celebrated Rome's birthday every year on the 21st April, as they still do. It is, beyond question, this feeling of eternity which has made, and still keeps, Rome unique. But in Roman eyes, Rome's youth did have one disadvantage: it implied lack of lineage of august ancestry. In the early days this did not matter very much: Rome was just a village, or union of villages, like others, Veii, or Alba Longa or Terracina; but when Rome became a ruling power, first in Italy then beyond its shores and finally the ruling power par excellence, it mattered very much indeed. In particular it mattered in Rome's dealings with three other nations, first the Greeks (and they, be it remembered, included the Greeks of what is now Southern Turkey, 'Asia Minor', one of the most fertile seed-beds of Greek genius), then the Egyptians, who seemed to be older than anyone, certainly older than Homer, and finally the Persians, or Parthians. With the Parthians Rome never came to any amicable understanding, and the fatal antagonism between the two races which lasted until both peoples went down before alien invaders in the seventh century of our era was one of the most destructive oppositions in the whole recorded history of mankind.

With Greece and Egypt relations were easier, if only because they both fell so easily to Roman arms. That made it all the more simple for Rome to appropriate some parts of their religions. It also tells how even from Persia Rome was to import myths, and still more vital how from the apparently negligible strip of land between Persia and Egypt Rome was to attract and assimilate the ideas and aspirations of an unimportant tribe or set of tribes called Hebrews. No one paid much attention to them, but it is worth recording that two of the ablest Romans who ever lived, namely Julius Caesar and Marcus Vipsanius Agrippa, Augustus' prime minister, did.

Mention of Julius Caesar brings us to the core of this book. The Romans are far more of an enigma than the Greeks, though with far fewer variations. We know the exterior features of many more Romans than we do of Greeks. The features of Augustus or of Nero are known to many; but not even the scholars would guarantee to describe just what Pericles or Socrates looked like. On the other hand whereas we know a great deal about the mind of Socrates and the mind of Pericles too, we know very little about how Romans thought; so much so that an English scholar recently told the Classical Association that any two books about Julius Caesar (and he himself has written one of the best) must be books about two different men.

In so far as Caesar was a quintessential Roman, he possessed (besides more questionable qualities) three very Roman attributes: he was proud, prompt and practical. His practicality urged him to some of his most enduring actions, such as the enlargement of the Forum and the reform of the calendar. His promptness has given us two of the best known *mots* of the Roman era. Having divorced his wife, before awaiting the official enquiry into an alleged nocturnal 'scandal' which had occurred in his own official residence, he had dismissed her, he said, because the wife of the High Priest, as he then was, must be above suspicion. That was in 62 BC. Fifteen years later, having conducted a victorious campaign in Asia Minor for a month and seven days he reported his success to the Senate in the immortal words: 'I came, I saw, I conquered — veni, vidi, vici'.

It was Caesar's pride that brought him to his doom; but it was his pride also that made him realize that what Rome needed was a pedigree. Really good mythology, in fact. No, not mythology; let the Greeks have that. Rome would go, and went, one better. 'No one', argued the practical Romans, 'likes being regarded as mythical: everybody is flattered by becoming legendary'. Thus it was that young Julius, when at the age of perhaps 33 he pronounced the funeral oration on his aunt Julia, told his hearers that he was descended on one side from Venus, the patron-goddess of Rome, and on the other from Aeneas, who had founded the city.

In this pronouncement of one of Rome's greatest sons we have the germ of Roman mythology. Both the goddess and the hero were, to put it kindly, obscure.

Obscure they would still be, had it not been for these practical Romans. Venus was really nobody — just a name, like most Roman deities. True, there was a temple down in the Forum to Venus Cloacina, Our Lady of the Sewers, a title which, until recent flights of the French literary genius, must have struck us as odd, the association of love and lavatories is still not regarded as being quite the thing by ordinary people. But Aphrodite! How different is she, the lovely, foam-born goddess, who rose from the azure main near Paphos in Cyprus, and hence was called the Paphian, the Cyprian, the goddess of all things bright and beautiful. Once assimilate Venus with Aphrodite and you have a goddess worth having. As Peter Croft shows us, in comparatively early days all the twelve Roman gods of any consequence had been assimilated to Greek counterparts — all except Apollo, who was so full of grace that no Roman deity could be found to match him, and so he is the only Greek god to retain his Greek name in the Roman pantheon.

Beside the Big Twelve there were as we read in these pages a whole host of godlets, swarms of them, presiding over nearly everything seen or unseen, felt or feared, gods of fertility, of the field, of the hearth, of the boundary, of the door, of the hinges, of the threshold. Gods of fever, gods of rust, gods of sowing, reaping, burning and dung-spreading.

If we ask what comfort these minigods gave to their adepts, the answer is none. They were not meant to. They were intended not to impart solace, but to promote terror. It is hard for us to comprehend how from first to last the Roman mind was saturated with superstition. That primitive Romans should have been afraid of the dark, or of lightning, would not to us seem odd; but what does strike us with bewilderment is that until the very latest days of the pagan Roman world sophisticated gentlemen, cynical authors even, would solemnly insert into a factual narrative such phrases as 'now the portents which foretold the elevation of 'so-and-so' were — anything from a donkey with two heads to a chicken with no liver, a tree withering here, an eagle flying there.

Although we know from Livy, who wrote in the days of Augustus, that in the heyday of the Republic 'enlightened' Romans were tired of all the mumbo jumbo of auspices and entrails, there were many others who went on taking the whole thing seriously. Ovid, the raffish poet who was more interested in earthly bodies than heavenly ones, designed a whole calendar, of which we possess the first six months, telling his smart readers just what must be done on what day, how, where and by whom, to keep Rome in with the gods. This subservience of the proud Romans to superstition makes the Roman quest for *salus*, that is 'health', or salvation all the more engrossing.

The Greeks, despite the Apostle Paul's compliment to the Athenians, were not what we would call a religious people. For them, gods and men were like masters and servants (some gods, such as Heracles and Asclepios, had started below stairs and worked their way up). If you treated them with deference, you could expect decent treatment in return. At least that was the theory, until people like Euripides pointed out that some of the gods were cads. But what did it matter? For the ordinary Hellene the world was full of all sorts of beautiful beings and things, nymphs, dryads, satyrs, Dionysus dispensing wine and ecstasy, mysteries, processions. (Ancient Greece had almost as many 'festivals' as modern Britain.) For more serious folk there was philosophy, the unending search for the temporal answer to the eternal questions. For the Roman there were no such solaces.

Thus it came about that the Romans sought their spiritual comfort elsewhere. First, in their national legends, and that brings us back to Aeneas. The origins of Rome are unexciting but undisputed. Like so many things Roman, the site of Rome was dictated by practical necessity. In the eighth century BC the chief power in northern Italy was the race we know as the Etruscans. We still do not know where they came from, nor, though we admire their arts, can we yet read their language. The river Tiber formed a boundary south of which Latin shepherds and herdsmen lived in humble settlements. The lowest point at which the Tiber was fordable (and the ford itself therefore a danger point for the Latins) was also the first place inland at

*This page*
A mosaic from Ephesus, Turkey, showing the head of Medusa.

*Following page*
One of Rome's great spring festivals was the Liberalia, honouring Liber, the god of vine growers, at a time when the latest vintage was ready for drinking. The celebration was common to all wine-producing countries at this season, so Liber came to be identified with the Greek god Dionysus or Bacchus, son of Jupiter and the Theban princess Semele. Bacchus, the name most used by the Romans, was commonly portrayed as in this mosaic from Paphos, Cyprus — a handsome. almost effeminate young man accompanied by a debauched Silenus and seated in a cart drawn by leopards. At the Liberalia Roman youths in their sixteenth year officially came of age and assumed the *toga virilis* — sign of a life free (*libera*) from parental authority.

which the river's southern bank is rendered defensible by two hills, each about 50 metres above sea level, namely the Palatine and the Capitol, as they were afterwards to be known. So it was on these two knolls that Rome came into beginning. Did Romulus exist? He may well have done, even if the wolf is mythical. The story that Cyrus the Persian was suckled by a bitch is no proof that he never lived. So how does Aeneas come in? The answer is the rather surprising one that over a very large part of Italy, that is from Naples southwards, the Greeks had got there long before the Romans. At a time when the inhabitants of Latium were rude goatherds and farmers, standing in awe of their mysterious, cruel but undoubtedly gifted Etruscan neighbours, the Greeks had established colonies imbued with their own civilization on many a smiling site in the south. Clearly therefore, if Rome was to have a respectable ancestry, a Trojan one would be smartest, because whoever may have won the Trojan War, it was obvious that Troy must have been there before the Greeks attacked it, or there would have been no war. (We now know that it was there a very, very long time before.)

So Aeneas, the dutiful son, the single-hearted soldier, this hero-figure becomes the founder of Rome. He is entertained by a shepherd on the Palatine. The shepherd is Evander, himself of Trojan origin. Thus is Rome's pedigree fabricated and authenticated.

Although Rome was now respectable, Rome was far from being religious, as we understand the term. True, on the Capitol there presided the Great Triad, Jupiter, Juno, assimilated with Hera, the wife of Zeus, and Minerva assimilated with Athena. Venerated here and there in the city below were the other minor, but still important, deities already mentioned. The Roman's relationship with them was, as already said, one of propitiatory dread. 'My will be done' was the Roman's attitude to religion and to those by whose means the gods might be wheedled into granting that will, even towards such sacrosanct Cinderellas as the Vestal Virgins, or the great Flamen Dialis, hedged about with so many cramping taboos that the office might remain vacant for years for lack of a candidate. The real bankruptcy of Roman ideas of deity was apparent to one and all when it became the custom (borrowed from the east) to 'deify' emperors. Augustus and Tiberius resisted it as far as they could, but the practice soon became established. It used to puzzle and shock Victorian moralists, because they unwittingly compared Roman concepts of godhead with their own; but the idea of a sublime, ineffable God was quite alien to Roman thought, as it was – again we turn to Paul's experience at Athens – to most of the Greeks as well. The word *divus* as applied posthumously to an emperor meant no more than the epithet 'most sacred' as applied to Hanoverian majesty, if as much.

Which brings us to the supreme interest and significance of Roman mythology, its importations from abroad. As will be seen from this book, these importations fall into three categories: philosophy, 'mystery' cults and monotheism. Of the philosophies, the two most important systems were those of the Epicureans and the Stoics. Both had started, almost simultaneously, in post-Alexandrine Athens, as manifestations of man's concern for himself as an *individual* not merely as a civic unit. Both set out to achieve *salus*, that is 'health' meaning spiritual health, but the methods that they advocated were very different. Whereas the Epicurean sought to dissociate himself from the world and all things worldly, the Stoic taught that there is a Providence which is active in the world, and that it is

man's stern duty to conform to the ordinances of this deity. This idea is not Greek at all, because the founder of Stoicism was not a Greek, but a Semite called Zeno, from Kitium in Cyprus. Thus we have in Stoicism the first and vital contact with the Semitic concept of the sublime, which was to be more mightily developed first in Judaism and then in Christianity.

Next come the foreign deities, the exotics from Asia and Egypt. The first alien deity to enter Rome was, as Peter Croft shows, Cybele, the Great Mother from Asia; and how strange was her advent, as a talisman against Rome's great enemy, Hannibal, and a successful talisman too. After her the gods of Asia arrive in an ever-increasing company. Then come the Egyptians, Isis in particular and Sarapis. These deities had the double advantage of being extremely ancient and also of inhabiting splendid and famous shrines in their unique homeland, where a bountiful river nourished mankind in a manner unparalleled in any other region of the known world. From time to time these alien cults caused scandals and were 'banished', but such was the solace (and excitement) they provided, so utter was their contrast with the dry-as-dust exercises of the indigenous religion, that they always made their way back, and rekindled their affecting liturgies. They were indeed what Milton rebukingly called them: 'gay religions, full of pomp and gold'.

Once the procession had started, it moved with everincreasing impetus, if only because Roman arms and Roman policy brought Rome into contact with so many exotic cults. As this book makes clear, there was as yet no sense of coercion in religions: you simply chose the one, or ones, which you felt would give you most comfort. Another point must be made – very few of the foreign liturgies prescribed a code of conduct. Stoicism did; and we must now mention three others which were in accord with Matthew Arnold's cardinal dictum that 'conduct is three-fourths of life', and they will lead us naturally to the third and most fruitful external graft onto the gnarled trunk of Roman religion, that is, monotheism. First and foremost comes Mithraism. Thanks to the great Belgian scholar Franz Cumont, we are now able to make a fairly accurate estimate, admirably mirrored in Dr Croft's pages, of the great influence which Mithras exercised throughout the empire. The vestiges of a Mithraum are still visible in the City of London; and as if to show how eclectic Roman religion was, this same shrine has yielded the finest head of Sarapis in existence. The heads of both gods from this site are now in the Guildhall Museum. There was at one time a tendency to overestimate the influence of Mithraism. 'If', says Renan, in his *Marc-Aurèle*, 'Christianity had been arrested in its growth by some mortal malady, the world would have been Mithraist'. Few would agree with that verdict today, but that Mithraism did bestow a real spiritual elevation, by imposing a real moral discipline, upon Roman belief and practice is undoubted.

Mithras was intimately associated with the sun. Sun-worship is an ancient rite. (It survives to this day in pagan manifestations of varying silliness on every available *plage*, with the accompaniment of the reintroduced burnt sacrifice of human flesh.) The Romans were first introduced to the sun cult in the days of Augustus, when that astute psychologist, as part of his campaign to rejuvenate Rome, imported the most ancient religious symbols then known – far older than anything those Greeks could produce – namely, two obelisks from Egypt. They were the first of the thirteen which now adorn the city. One, originally quarried at Aswan between 1232 and 1200 BC, now stands in the Piazza del Popolo, the other, dating from the early years of the sixth century BC, on Montecitorio. Both are inscribed by their imperial donor as 'gifts to the sun' — correctly enough, because as Pliny knew, obelisks were regarded by the Egyptians as symbolizing the sun's rays. Augustus had imported them for political reasons; but by introducing these 'gifts to the sun' he was in fact preparing the way for the worship of the 'Unconquered Sun'. After the marriage of the Emperor Septimius Severus to Julia Domna, the daughter of the priest of the sun god at Emesa, this was to become increasingly fashionable in Rome, until by the end of the third century it was established as to all intents and purposes the official state religion. Augustus of course, could not have foreseen this, nor would he have approved of it. His aim was to revivify the old Roman religion, the 'gods of earth and altar' so touchingly portrayed on his Altar of Peace, itself one of the most moving religious sculptures ever created. Then, too, Augustus had at his service one of the most spiritually minded poets who ever sang, namely Virgil. It is largely due to the Augustan policy of 'renewal' that the old Roman religion did contrive to survive for so long. With the sun, monotheism had come to Rome, and so would ultimately make it the hearth and centre as it still is of a monotheistic faith which for 300 years Rome did all in her power to eradicate, namely Christianity.

The Christian Faith sprang from a Jewish matrix. Exactly when the Jews reached Rome it is not possible to say. That they were 'expelled' from the city in 139 BC we do know. By the end of the Republican period they were a numerous community, and a very valuable one. The Jews were not only worshippers of a single God, but they claimed that He was the One and Only God, and that all men ought to obey his commands, led and enlightened by His chosen servants. Here was something entirely novel in religious experience. It was naturally unpopular in easy-going pagan circles, but it did stand up to practical tests. These Jews, with their strict rules of conduct —

the Ten Commandments they called them — supplemented by practical regulations for the living of everyday life, including honesty in commerce, really were more trustworthy than many a loose-living Gentile. It therefore happened that while their exclusiveness made them unpopular as it has often done since, their standards and methods made them respected by those whose respect was worth having, as it still does. Not all those who admired them joined their community; but they emulated their precepts.

From among such folk there finally appeared what was at first regarded as a mere 'splinter-group' of Judaism. Soon however it became clear that the Christians were nothing of the sort; they claimed to be the apostles of an universal Faith, nay more, of the universal Faith. This brought upon them violent antagonism, first from the Jews, who regarded the Christians both as blasphemers (for exalting a man to Godhead) and as renegades (for proclaiming that the spiritual patrimony of Jewry might be appropriated by any who cared to partake of it), and then from the Romans, who regarded 'King Jesus' as a subversive rival.

Thus was played out the long, triumphant tragedy. In the end, it was both Caesar and Christ who were the victors, aided not a little by the Unconquered Sun, who had done so much to shed the light of Salvation amid the family of the first Christian emperor, Constantine.

Peter Croft has undertaken to retell this fascinating story. It is not only fascinating, but in fact timely. The subject which his book expounds is the evolution of Roman religion from a hut on the Palatine to the Basilica of Saint Peter's from the Forum to the ends of the earth. The foundation, in fact, of the era of European civilization which is now drawing to a close. (No era ever thinks it will draw to a close, but they all do.) What is to succeed it we still cannot discern. It is all the more necessary therefore to have a sure grasp of our own civilization as we possess it.

*Stewart Perowne*

GENVS·VNDE
LATINVM

# BEFORE THE DAWN

CHAPTER

I

The Romans' firm belief that they were of Trojan origin was based on the myth of Aeneas, the son of an otherwise obscure Trojan prince, Anchises, and the goddess of love, Venus. Such unions were not unknown in the histories of aristocratic families, and the Julians, represented by such men of distinction as Julius Caesar and his great-nephew Augustus, claimed that their *gens* or clan was descended directly from Aeneas himself. In this fresco from Rome's Palazzo Farnese the consummation of Venus's love for Anchises is vividly portrayed by Caracci and neatly expressed in the words of the poet Virgil – *genus unde Latinum* – 'the origins of the Romans'.

*Above*
Troy stands on the narrow strip of water that forms the barrier between Greece and Turkey. On these plains, seen here from the crumbling remains of the once-proud city, was fought the famous war between the Greeks and the Trojans, ostensibly over the rape of Helen, a Greek queen, by the Trojan prince Paris. Paris had been granted this privilege by Venus when he awarded her the golden apple as a prize for beauty in a competition held on Mount Ida. By doing so Paris inevitably incurred the displeasure of the other two contestants, Juno, the queen of the gods, and Minerva, or Athene, as the Greeks called her, who arranged for him to be killed in the war.

*Right*
The Trojan War continued indecisively for ten years and was eventually ended by a Greek trick, the Wooden Horse. The Horse, with Greek soldiers in its belly, was left on the plains of Troy while the rest of the Greeks sailed away — to return the next night after the Trojans had been tricked by a Greek confidence man into thinking that the Horse would protect Troy if it were taken inside the city. It was, and the Greeks inside it let themselves out in the darkness and opened the gates of Troy to their returning forces. This wall painting from Pompeii shows the Horse being brought into the city amid excited crowds.

*Below*

Episodes from the sack of Troy are depicted on this marble relief of the first century A D found at Bovillae near Albano in Italy, now in the Capitoline Museum at Rome. The inscription tells us that the scenes are taken from a work (now lost) of Stesichorus, a lyric poet who flourished in Sicily in the sixth century BC. One scene shows Aeneas with Ascanias and Anchises and bears the legend 'Aeneas setting out for the Western Land with his family'. From this it has been inferred that the myth of Aeneas's migration to Italy goes back at least to the time of Stesichorus. But this has been doubted by recent scholars.

*Right*

Troy has been destroyed. Aeneas has been saved by his mother Venus, who has told him that he must leave Troy and found another city overseas. In this splendid marble group, now in the Borghese Gallery at Rome, Bernini has portrayed the piety of Aeneas, who carries on his shoulders his aged father, paralyzed by Jupiter in revenge for his affair with Venus. In his emaciated hands Anchises supports the symbols of Troy, the Penates or household gods. Behind them stumbles the young Ascanias, carrying a torch not only to illuminate his father's path but also to ensure the continuity of the spirit of Troy.

*Left*

The sun breaks through storm clouds over the bay of Carthage to bathe the ruined columns of the Roman city. Carthage was originally founded as a Phoenician colony and trading post on the North African coast, near what is now Tunis. Here Aeneas and the survivors of the Trojan War landed in their quest for a new homeland, after being blown off course by a storm prompted by Juno, who was determined to destroy the last vestiges of a race she hated. But Destiny decreed otherwise. Carthage, a city dedicated to Juno, was fated to be destroyed by the heirs of Aeneas. In fact, the city was totally razed by Rome after a triple series of wars, the most famous of which is for ever associated with Hannibal.

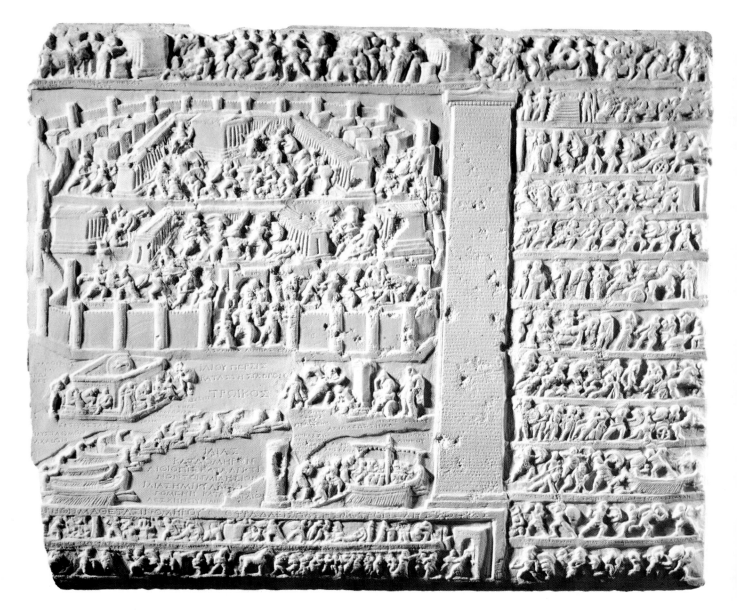

*Left*

This is an illustration from the *Codex Romanus*, a manuscript written in the fifth or sixth century AD, now in the Vatican Library. Textually, perhaps, it is less than accurate, but visually it is one of the most attractive of the editions of Virgil's *Aeneid*. The ships of Aeneas are tossed by a storm, personified by the malignant figures above them, while the hero raises pious hands to pray that he should not suffer such an ignominious death. The crews seem splendidly placid amid the tumoil around them, and the presence of the sea monsters waiting with beady eyes for their prey — in vain. Neptune came to the rescue and calmed his sea.

*Below*

Aeneas is welcomed to Carthage by Queen Dido outside the Temple of Juno. He is attended by his faithful companion, Achates. The pair had set out, after their two ships reached land safely, to explore and find the rest of their comrades who had been dispersed by the storm in the fleet's other five ships. While searching they met Venus, disguised as a huntress (centre), and she not only soothed their anxieties but told them where they were and some essential facts about Dido. In this illumination from a manuscript in the

British Museum, Venus points heaven-
wards to seven swans, symbols of Aeneas's
seven ships. The other five are shown
sailing safely into the harbour at rear.

*Above*
This mosaic now in the British Museum
delightfully epitomizes the legend of
Aeneas and Dido, a hesitant man and a
determined woman. Aeneas had left Troy
seven years before. He was weary and
often despaired of fulfilling his destiny,
the founding of a new Troy. He had been
received in Carthage with enthusiasm by
its queen and the temptation to linger
was great — too great to resist. He was
flattered, too, by the attention Dido
showed him, an attention which turned
to admiration, love, and eventually to an
unconquerable passion. The hunt shown
here provided the climax of the story.

*Right*
The act of consummation. During the
hunt Dido and Aeneas shelter in a cave
from a storm. The whole episode was
engineered by Juno and Venus from
different motives of hate and affection.
As Virgil graphically wrote, 'The sky
connived at the union, the lightning
flared, on their mountain peak nymphs
raised their cry. On that day were sown
the seeds of suffering and death'. The
news spread and Aeneas was recalled to
his destiny by Jupiter, who sent his
messenger Mercury with a curt reminder.
This illustration is also to be found in the
*Codex Romanus*.

Postq̃ fata uolent: nec iam datur ulla uoluptas.
Conscenditq; pyram: dixitq; nouissima uerba.
At uitam infelix multo cum sanguine fudit;

# P· VIRGILII MARO
# NIS AENEIDOS
# LIB·IIII·

VENIVNTHERAIADVMINCVMVIRCOLOSCIRIEIAIA
IIMPVSAITDIVSICCIDIVSCVIIALIAIANII·
ANIIFORISSVBIIONONVCIIVSNONCOLORVNVS·
NONCONIEINIMANSIRICOMMISIDEICIVSADHILVM
EIRABIIIIIRAGODADAIMINIMMIOAQVIIVIDIRI
NICMOAINAIISONANIMIIIIAIAISINVMINİQVANDO·

---

*Left*

The final scene in the story of Dido's love for Aeneas was her death by her own hand. On this exquisite page at the beginning of Book IV of the *Aeneid* the scribe has painted both the beginning and end of this tragedy, the entry into the cave during the hunt and the suicide on the funeral pyre. The events in between are poignantly told by Virgil: how love turned to passion, despair, and ultimately hate, while Dido tried to stop Aeneas from leaving her. As one modern commentator has written, 'The story of Dido has haunted the imagination of Europe, drawing tears from saints and sinners, from St Augustine in the fourth century as from Anatole France in the twentieth'.

*Right*

This painting from Modena by a minor Renaissance artist ingeniously presents the events of the whole of Book V of the *Aeneid*, 871 lines of poetry. It depicts the return of Aeneas to Sicily after leaving Carthage, an interval of calm between the tragedy of Dido's suicide, still unknown to Aeneas, and the hero's dramatic descent to the Underworld. In the centre games are held near Anchises' tomb, on the anniversary of his death at Drepanum in the north of Sicily: sailing and foot races, boxing and archery, followed by an equestrian exercise of young men. In the background a snake glides from the tomb, where it consumes the sacrifices, an omen of dubious significance. Iris ascends her rainbow after persuading the Trojan women to burn their fleet and end their wanderings. They are thwarted (foreground), and Venus asks Neptune to give her son a safe voyage to Italy, which is marred only by the loss of the helmsman, Palinurus, seen tumbling overboard, an innocent victim to placate the sea god. Dominating the whole is a sugar-cake Segesta, the city Aeneas founded in Sicily.

*Left*

Aeneas has landed in Italy at Cumae near Naples to seek the aid of the Sibyl, Apollo's priestess and prophetess, for his promised journey into Hades, the land of the dead. Achates again accompanies his leader, and the Sibyl, less frenzied than Virgil describes her, carries a branch in her hand, because she usually wrote her prophecies on leaves which were scattered by winds through her cave. The temple at rear belies Virgil's account of a vast cave as the Sibyl's seat. But excavations at Cumae have revealed a long gallery ending in a large chamber similar to the galleries of Tiryns and Mycenae in Greece — a clear link with a Trojan past.

P·VIRGILII MARO
NIS AENEIDOS
LIBER·VI·
IC FATVR
LACHRY
MANS ♀
CLASSIQ·
IMMITTIT HABENAS·

*Above*
Aeneas sets off for the Underworld with the Sibyl, who acts as guide, having had the advantage of a previous trip. Charon ferries them across the Styx, the river which separates this world from the next, although their weight almost sinks a boat accustomed to hold insubstantial phantoms. Once across, they face the three-headed dog, Cerberus, who guards the entrance to Hades, and pacify him with drugs. Eventually they reach the Elysian Fields, where Anchises carries out his task of revealing the future to his son.

Here he points out the souls of future Romans destined to achieve fame in their country's service, an opportunity for Virgil to aid his emperor's propaganda about the greatness of Rome.

*Right*
The Temple of Mars Ultor, the avenging god of war (centre) was built by Augustus to fulfil a vow made before his victory at Philippi over the murderers of his kinsman and predecessor Julius Caesar. An open space or forum surrounded the temple, which contained statues of Mars and Venus as well as an object of special

veneration, Caesar's own sword. In this way Augustus contrived to remind his countrymen of the two legends about Rome's origins: that the Julian *gens* was descended from Venus through Aeneas, and that Mars was the father of the twins, Romulus and Remus, who founded a city on the site of Rome.

*Above*

The last six books of Virgil's epic describe Aeneas's difficulties and ultimate success in founding a colony in Latium in Italy. But although he was received kindly on arrival by Latinus, king of the Latins, the prospect of the new colony was unwelcome to Latinus's neighbours, and when the king offered Aeneas the hand of his only child, Lavinia, in marriage, this was too much for Turnus, the prince to whom she was already betrothed. War was inevitable, but Aeneas found an unexpected ally in Evander, a Greek who had recently settled on the future site of Rome and was hard pressed by the same enemies. On the left Venus arms Aeneas with new weapons especially made for him by Vulcan. On the right Evander welcomes Aeneas from his ship.

*Following page*

The site of Lavinium, Aeneas's colony, was revealed to him in a dream by the river god Tiber, who told him to claim the spot where he found a white sow with a litter of thirty young. In this marble relief Aeneas, still accompanied by Achates, is about to sacrifice the sow to Juno, who had tried in vain to stop his arrival in Italy. In the shrine behind him are the household gods, the Penates, which Aeneas had brought from Troy. The relief is from the Ara Pacis Augustae in Rome.

# IN THE BEGINNING

CHAPTER
## II

The father of Romulus and Remus was Mars and their mother was Rhea Silvia, a princess of Alba Longa, a city which was settled from Lavinium by Ascanias, Aeneas's son. Numitor, the king of Alba, was expelled by his younger brother, Amulius, who butchered his nephews and made his niece Rhea Silvia a Vestal Virgin, ostensibly to honour her but in fact to stop her having any children. The precaution was useless because she was made pregnant by Mars. When her twins were born, the king ordered them to be thrown into the Tiber. But the Tiber was in flood, the babies' basket floated, and when the water subsided the twins were left in the reeds, where they were found and suckled by a wolf. These incidents are portrayed on this ancient altar.

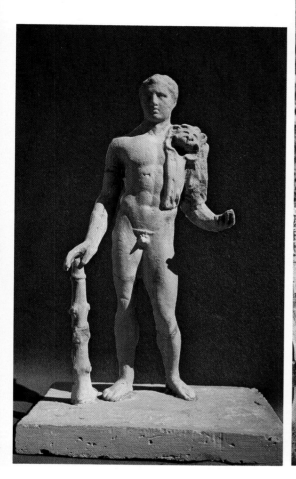

The Flemish artist Rubens has depicted the moment when Romulus and Remus are discovered by the king's herdsman, Faustulus, while the river god leans against the source of the Tiber, accompanied by a demurely seventeenth-century nymph. The tree in the foreground is a fig – Rubens knew his mythology! Faustulus gave the boys to his wife, Larentia, to nurse. The name Larentia is assumed to mean the mother of the Lares, the deified ancestors and guardian gods of a community. Romulus and Remus were the ancestors of the Roman people and so on their death became Lares. The boys grew up to lead their fellows in several escapades which came to the attention of their grandfather, Numitor. Amulius was killed, the people of Alba told the true facts, and Numitor restored to his throne.

*Left*

This splendid bronze of the wolf which suckled Romulus and Remus is now appropriately housed on the Capitoline Hill, the centre of Rome. In fact the wolf is antique, an Etruscan work of the fifth century BC, and the twins were made by a fifteenth-century Florentine artist, Pollaiuolo. The Roman historian Livy tells us that the wolf suckled them on the spot by the River Tiber where she found them, which was later marked by a fig tree, the ficus Ruminalis. The goddess Rumina was a primeval goddess of nursing whose name is said to be connected with *ruma*, 'a breast'. The exposure of the twins sounds suspiciously like the early history of Cyrus, king of Persia, or the myth of Neleus and Pelias, twin sons of Poseidon, who were suckled respectively by a bitch and a mare. It is a neat way of accounting for the arrival of a new force lacking background or family.

*Above*

Hercules, shown here in a Roman statue from Manisa, in present-day Turkey, featured early in Rome's history. As one of his twelve Labours Hercules had to fetch the cattle of Geryon from the west and bring them back to Greece. He paused at the Tiber on his way and while he was asleep a local giant named Cacus stole some of the cows. Hercules managed to recover them and killed Cacus with his club. Recognizing the hero, Evander, the Greek who was the site's first colonist, hailed him as a god. Hercules promptly built himself an altar – the Ara Maxima – and sacrificed one of Geryon's cattle.

*Above right*

The River Tiber played a big part in the legends of early Rome. As a result of its association with the miraculous survival of Romulus and Remus the neighbouring hills were chosen for the first Roman settlements. The most famous legend connected with the river is that of Horatius Cocles, who with two companions faced the entire Etruscan army on the one bridge left across the Tiber until it was destroyed in his rear, a legend immortalized in Macaulay's *Lays of Ancient Rome*. The Ponte Sant'Angelo here shown was originally built by the Emperor Hadrian and later decorated with statues of angels by Bernini.

*Following pages*

Romulus found difficulty in populating his new settlement of Rome, particularly because of a shortage of women. He therefore invited the neighbouring tribe of the Sabines to a festival, and at a given signal the young women spectators were seized. Panic was followed by bitter fighting between Romans and Sabines. The battle was finally brought to an end by the intervention of the women. Sabine by birth and Roman by marriage, they naturally considered stalemate better than victory by either side. In this picture the French artist David has shown little historical knowledge, but that may have been what his public expected and liked.

*Above*

Castor and Pollux, seen here in mosaics from Paphos in Cyprus, were the twin sons of Leda and Jupiter – and known as Dioscuri by the Greeks. Traditionally, they made their first appearance on the Roman scene in 496 BC. The Romans were at war with the Latins, who were supporting the Tarquins, the deposed kings of Rome, in their effort to regain power. The two armies met in battle at Lake Regillus near Tusculum and in the course of the equally matched engagement the Roman commander, Postumius, secured Castor's help by vowing to build a temple to him if he were successful. It was commonly believed that both Castor and Pollux had fought for the Romans and afterwards brought news of the victory to Rome. The brothers also apparently assisted at subsequent Roman battles. In later times they were identified with the constellation Gemini by the Roman poet Ovid.

*Below*

The statue of the dying Gaul, now in the Capitoline Museum in Rome, recalls the invasions into central Italy by the Gauls in the fourth century BC. As they swept south from the Anio, Rome was in peril, and tradition has it that only the cackling of the sacred geese saved the Capitoline Hill from capture. The legends are preserved in Livy's *History* and archaeologists confirm the occupation.

*Left*

The Forum at Rome was not only the political centre of the city, but also the scene of many of the early myths unfolded in this book. Across it and up to the Capitoline Hill ran the main street, the Via Sacra. In the foreground are the three columns of the Temple of the Dioscuri and the remains of the tiny Temple of Vesta. The three Corinthian columns on a massive podium (right) are all that is left of the Temple of Castor and Pollux, rebuilt and dedicated in 6 AD by Tiberius, the heir apparent of the reigning Emperor Augustus. The temple was on the site of the original building vowed by Postumius at the Battle of Lake Regillus and dedicated by his son, Livy tells us, on 15th July, 484 BC, the anniversary of the engagement. The temple was built on this site because it was next to the spring — the Lacus Juturnae — where traditionally Castor and Pollux were seen watering their horses after bringing the news of the battle to Rome. The open space beyond is the area of the Lacus Curtius, in early times a marsh though dry by the time of Augustus. According to one legend, the Sabine leader Mettius Curtius rode his horse into this swamp while being pursued by the Romans, but managed to escape.

*Left*

The incident depicted in this picture by the fifteenth-century artist Domenico Morone occurred in the same year, 508 BC, as Horatius's defence of the bridge, and concerned the same enemy, who were now besieging Rome. Gaius Mucius, a young aristocrat, volunteered to enter the Etruscan camp and assassinate Lars Porsenna, their king. Unfortunately, he attacked the wrong man, a secretary, who was sitting by the king. Taken prisoner, Mucius thrust his right hand into the fire burning on a nearby altar, to show the king his disregard of physical pain. Impressed, the king released him and, through fear of similar attempts on his life, negotiated peace with the Romans. In this way Mucius earned the nickname of Scaevola or Left-Handed, the name of a family distinguished in later Roman history.

CVMAEA

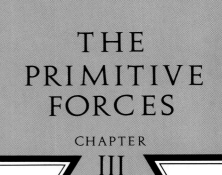

THE
PRIMITIVE
FORCES
CHAPTER
III

*Left*
The Sibyl of Cumae played a significant
part in the myths of Rome. Michelangelo
immortalized her on the ceiling of the
Sistine Chapel, here, as a pagan
prophetess, who with her sisters balances
the Old Testament prophets and reminds
the popes of the fusion of the two
cultures in Christianity. It was the Sibyl
who brought to Tarquinius Superbus,
Rome's last king, those invaluable books
of prophecy which at first he refused on
economic grounds. Eventually he was
persuaded by an unusual sales technique
into purchasing the last three books for
the price of the original nine, after the
Sibyl had burnt the other six. They were
carefully preserved and consulted on
historic occasions.

*This page*
Saturnus was by origin and doubtful
definition an Italian god of agriculture
who had lived on earth as a king in Italy,
presiding over a Golden Age. He later
came to be identified as Time, in which
guise he appears here, with his wheel and
a child in his lap representing the New
Year, in the fourteenth-century
campanile of the Cathedral in Florence.
He was also identified with the Greek
Cronus, father of Jupiter, who overthrew
him and usurped his power. His chief
festival was the Saturnalia, which began
on 17th December each year and in its
riotous licence bore some resemblance
to the less religious side of our Christmas
festivities.

*Left*
The Roman Forum is seen at dawn. In the foreground are the eight Ionic columns of the Temple of Saturnus standing high above vaults where the bronze money of the senatorial treasury was stored — the Romans frequently used their temples for more than religious purposes. This temple stood at the foot of the Capitol and so symbolized, if not deliberately, the subservience of the old order of Saturnus to that of Jupiter whose imposing temple stood on the Capitol. The present columns belong to a reconstruction of the fourth century AD but tradition says that the earliest Temple of Saturnus was built in 497 BC on the site of an even more ancient altar to the god.

*Right*
The legends of the Greek Pan, spirit of the mountains and woods, are numerous. Known to the Romans as Faunus, he retained the lecherous qualities of Pan, symbolized by his lower half being that of a goat, as in this mosaic from Paphos. In his honour was held annually the Lupercalia, most primitive of Roman rituals. Aristocratic youths ran naked up and down the Via Sacra, striking bystanders with strips of goatskins. Later the ceremony changed character until it came to be thought of as a fertility rite, but it is probable that they were originally impersonating wolves — *lupi* — menacing Rome's flocks.

*Left*
Pompeii was a sophisticated urban society in 79 AD when the city was destroyed by the eruption of Mount Vesuvius. Among evidence of this revealed by excavations is a vivid bronze of Faunus that occupied a prominent position in what was the *atrium* of a well-to-do family's house. The original statue is now in the Naples Museum; this modern cast has been placed on the original spot. If the proximity of Vesuvius constantly reminded the Pompeians of primitive forces better recognized than ignored, no god could have been more evocative of this than Faunus.

Portunus, the god of communications,
was an ancient Latin god. Virgil represents
him in the Sicilian games instituted by
Aeneas as giving one of the ships a
helping hand. He seems to have been
considered variously as god of the
harbour – *portus* – or of the gate –
*porta*. The latter has caused some
confusion with Janus, god of doorways.
A festival in his honour – the Portunalia
– was held annually in August on the
anniversary of the dedication of his
temple. This building may or may not
have been Portunus's temple, but it does
stand where one Roman author tells us
his temple stood, near the Aemilian
Bridge, beside the Tiber. It is one of the
few pre-Augustan buildings in Rome

to be well preserved.

*Right and above*
In the centre of a primitive house was the
hearth, where a fire was kept burning for
cooking and warmth. Like water and air,
fire was a symbol of life, and it inspired
the cult of Vesta, introduced to Rome
by Numa. Vesta's temples were usually
round, symbolizing the hearth they
embraced, like this one (above), which is at
Tivoli, not far from Rome, situated high
above the River Anio. Ovid tells us that
Vesta was the daughter of Saturnus and
Ops, goddess of the harvest. She was a
virgin, as were her ministers, six young
women of aristocratic birth who tended
the sacred flame. Vesta's temple in Rome
was built next to the Regia, traditional

home of the king as chief priest or Pontifex Maximus (left). These graceful columns and part of the wall are all that remain in the Forum of a later restoration, dominated by the eastern side of the Palatine Hill, visible in the background.

*Right*
Janus was a unique god who appeared only in Roman mythology. As god of doorways, he faced both outwards and inwards, and was therefore commonly depicted with two heads, as on this coin. Janus was also the god of beginnings and gave his name to the first month of each year. In addition, the first day of every month was sacred to him. His cult was established when Numa, the second king

of Rome, built him a temple near the Senate House in the Forum. In times of war its gates were always left open, and so turbulent was Rome's history that Livy records only three occasions on which they were closed.

*Above*
The Lares were the twin sons of Mercury and the nymph Lara, and as Mercury was the protector of travellers it was natural to find shrines to his sons at crossroads, those places of vital decision for the traveller. In addition, a small shrine or Lararium usually graced a Roman house. The one here, found at Pompeii, shows the two Lares dancing, with upheld drinking horns. The snake beneath may symbolize the spirit of the dead.

*Left*
Rivers in Italy are usually powerful forces, especially in spring after the winter snows have melted; no wonder, then, that they were deified. At Rome the River Tiber was annually placated on 14th May when *argei* — bundles of rushes resembling men bound hand and foot — were carried to the river by priests called *pontifices*, 'bridge builders', whose task must originally have been to appease the river when a bridge was thrown over it, rendering it inferior to man. This statue represents another river god, the Nile, as is clear from the sphinx on which he reclines; it is in the piazza of the Capitol.

*Above*
If rivers could be represented as gods, why not towns and countries? Temples were built to Rome as a goddess, and she was often associated with the emperor himself. This mosaic from a villa at Piazza Armerina in central Sicily portrays Africa as a handsome woman. Surrounded by her animals, including the mythical phoenix (left), she holds in her left arm a horn, symbol of plenty, taken from an elephant, while her right hand clasps a palm tree.

*Following pages*
The Roman instinct for seeing divinity in nature is beautifully expressed in this relief of Earth personified as a mature but graceful mother with twins on her knee. The babies may represent Romulus and Remus, for the relief comes from the Altar of Peace — the Ara Pacis — dedicated by Augustus to herald the end of wars throughout the Roman Empire. The relief is embellished with plants and flowers and other signs of the earth's fruitfulness, and air and water are also personified, in the sea serpent and the swan.

The Romans were an earthy people, with
many agricultural divinities. Pomona, the
goddess of fruit trees, was important
enough to have her own priests, *flamines*;
the two Pales were deities of stock
breeding. There were Consus and Ops,
gods of storing away and plenty; Flora,
who saw to the flowering of crops, was
saluted at a festival of games, the Ludi
Florales, each April. And Robigus, god
of rust, brought mildew to crops if not
appeased with a sacrifice of a sheep and
a dog. These two pictures illustrate the
personification which with the Romans
was the first step to deification. One is a
fresco of Spring from a villa wall in
Stabiae *right*; the other, from a Cyprus
house, is a mosaic of fruitful Autumn *left*.

*Below left*
At Praeneste, in the hills southeast of
Rome, there still stands the terrace of
the famous shrine and oracle of the
goddess Fortuna. It was probably from
here that her cult was introduced into
Rome by King Servius Tullius. She had
no festival but several shrines under
various titles, such as Virilis, or
Muliebris — of men, or of women.
One such shrine, Livy records, was built
to commemorate the time in 488 BC
when the traitor Coriolanus was
persuaded by his wife and mother to
lead away the army which he had brought
to attack Rome. Fortuna was by origin
probably a deity of agriculture, where
good fortune may play as large a part as
hard work; she was accepted in Rome as
a goddess of luck.

*Above*
Flora as goddess of flowering crops was
surrounded in the imagination of poets
by all that was beautiful. Her attendants
in this fresco from Pompeii are the three
Graces, daughters of Jupiter,
personifications of loveliness, who
perhaps were originally goddesses of
vegetation. Resting gracefully on each
other's shoulders, they hold flowers
in their hands. In legends, too, they
were fit companions for Venus and
rejoiced in such euphonious names as
Thaleia, 'flowering', Euphrosyne, 'joy',
and Aglaia, 'radiant'.

*Right*
The Capitol as it appears today. Few
visitors to Rome fail to make the
pilgrimage up the sloping ramp to the
glorious piazza of Michelangelo that now
covers both the citadel and the religious
centre of the ancient city. Guarding the
ramp are two huge statues of Castor and
Pollux from the Theatre of Pompey,
reminders of their role in Rome's

mythology. The modern buildings
around the piazza cover the Tabularium,
the former public record office, and the
Temple of Jupiter, Juno and Minerva,
and house a valuable collection of
*objets d'art* from Rome's past. Against
the balustrade of the Senatorial Palace
(rear) two river gods, the Nile and the
Tiber, frame a small statue personifying
Rome.

THE
ESTABLISH-
MENT

CHAPTER

IV

Jupiter was the god of sky and weather and the Ides of each month were set aside for his worship. On that day Jupiter's priest, the Flamen Dialis, would lead a white ewe lamb along the Via Sacra up to the Capitoline Hill and sacrifice it in front of his temple. As a sky god, Jupiter had agricultural interests, which included the inauguration of the Vinalia, or feast of wine on 19th August. Another festival, on 23rd December, celebrated the recovery of light from the darkness of winter solstice. Jupiter shared a vast temple on the Capital with Juno and Minerva, both females. Here the influence of Greek myths played havoc with native Italian traditions, where it is highly doubtful if Jupiter had any connection with either lady. In the course of time, however, Jupiter was identified with the Greek Zeus, Juno with his wife Hera, and Minerva with Athene his daughter, patroness of craftsmen. *Far right* the marriage of Jupiter and Juno is shown in a detail of a Fresco found at Pompeii.

*Right*

Juno was worshipped under many titles, among them Sospita, Lucina, Sororia, Iuga, Mater Regina, all showing her concern for women in various stages of their lives, as preserver, goddess of childbirth, puberty, and marriage, and queen mother. She played a part in many Roman myths, and it was she who did all in her power to prevent Aeneas's voyage from Troy to Italy. Livy tells us that her worship was brought from the Etruscan city of Veii to Rome in 396 BC. This queenly statue of the goddess is now in the Vatican.

*Above*

Minerva was the other goddess who with Juno shared the temple of Jupiter Optimus Maximus on the Capitol at Rome. According to tradition the Palladium, her sacred effigy, was brought from Troy to Italy by Aeneas and kept by later generations in the Temple of Vesta, an essential security for the welfare of Rome. In later times she was honoured at the five-day March festival called Quinquatrus. This originally had nothing to do with her — a good example of the way in which confusion arose among the Romans over half-understood traditions and anniversaries. This head of Minerva is from a theatre in Turkey.

*Left*
From the foam of this bay near Paphos in Cyprus, according to one legend, Venus sprang, fully formed. When she came to land she took refuge in the myrtle trees, which have been sacred to her ever since. Her worship was popular throughout the island, which points to the Eastern origin of her cult. Thanks to Greek influence, it spread to Sicily, where an important temple was built to her on Mount Eryx. During the early wars against Carthage the Romans gained control of Sicily, and after a consultation of the Sibylline Books, built a temple in Rome to Venus Erucina, which was dedicated in 215 BC.

*Below*
Stories about Venus, confused with those about the Greek Aphrodite, figure largely in the poems of Ovid. Inevitably the prostitutes of Rome adopted Venus as their cult figure, and honoured her with a festival on 23rd April, a date that was also that of the Vinalia, a wine festival honouring Jupiter. This statuette of Venus in painted marble is from Pompeii, where the goddess was recognized by the citizens as their official protectress.

*Right*
Romans traditionally derived their descent from Venus through Aeneas and from Mars through Romulus, a link that was perhaps not fortunate — for Mars was traditionally the paramour of Venus, although neither remained exclusively devoted to the other. In this fresco at Pompeii Cupid watches Mars and Venus. To the Romans Mars was certainly a god of war — and therefore the horse was sacred to him as a necessary aid in warfare. Mars also had agricultural functions, and the Roman calendar originally started with his month, March, while his principal festivals were celebrated in the spring, clear indications of his importance to farmers.

*Following pages*
The allegorical *Birth of Venus* by Botticelli is deservedly one of the most famous paintings of the Renaissance. Venus is the Roman name for the Greek goddess of love, Aphrodite. She played an important role in Roman myth as the mother of Aeneas, founder of the Roman race and ancestor of the Caesars. It is surprising that her worship was not important at Rome until the times of the Caesars. Naturally Julius made her temple the centrepiece of his Forum and gave her the appropriate title of Genetrix — mother. An imposing temple was dedicated to Venus and Rome jointly by the Emperor Hadrian in 135 AD, symbolically underlining their association.

SANDRO BOTT
FIORENTINO
NASCITA

Apollo was a Greek god who did not even change his name when he came to Rome. He was widely worshipped in the Greek-speaking world, and it is not surprising to find abundant evidence of his cult in Italy before the Romans became supreme, especially among the Etruscans. The terracotta statue is in the Villa Giulia, the Etruscan museum in Rome, and is one of several such cult statues from various parts of Etruria. Apollo is often shown as a handsome young man with rather soft features and a splendid head of hair. His oracle at Delphi in Greece, Livy tells us, was often consulted by the Etruscan kings.

*Right*
Augustus had a particular devotion to Apollo and built him a temple on the Palatine next to his own home, on this site, later occupied by the Stadium of Domitian. The temple was one of the most magnificent in Rome, and beneath its great statue of the god were stored the prophecies which replaced the original Sibylline Books destroyed in the Civil Wars between Marius and Sulla. The Centenary Games held by Augustus in 17 BC were, unusually, dedicated to Apollo, and the poet Horace was commissioned to write a hymn — which

has survived — to be sung by a choir of boys and girls from noble families in honour of the god and his sister Diana. From this time onwards Apollo's cult practically rivalled that of Jupiter.

*Below*
Temples to Apollo were common throughout Italy. This temple in Pompeii was built in the reign of Nero, shortly before the destruction of the city in 79 AD. It was on the site of a temple of

*Right*
Diana, originally a goddess of forests, was often portrayed as a huntress, as in this statue. In early Italian history she had been the principal deity of the Latin League, a free association of tribes and cities in central Italy. Her shrine was a sacred grove near Aricia and the modern village of Nemi, a few miles southeast of Rome. Even before Rome became head of the League, a place was found for Diana among the city's deities and a temple was built to her on the Aventine. According to Livy, her worship was established by King Servius Tullius, and its adherents practised a Greek ritual.

pre-Roman times and testifies to the active influence of the Greeks in Southern Italy. Games, too, were held annually at Rome in Apollo's honour, a tradition originating from the Second Punic War. These games were characterized by dramatic performances in the Greek manner and combats of gladiators, a native Italian tradition. These were also popular in Pompeii, where there was a large amphitheatre for their display, one of the oldest known.

*Below*
If Livy is right that Diana's earliest worshippers in Rome practised a Greek ritual, then the way was open to identify her with the Greek Artemis, sister of Apollo, also a goddess of hunting. Both Diana and Artemis helped women by giving them children too, so it was not a big step to portray Diana as a fertility goddess. Here she is portrayed in a cult statue from Ephesus which unashamedly reveals this function.

*Left*
The Romans evolved no theories of their own about life after death but borrowed their beliefs first from the Etruscans and later from the Greeks. Abundant Etruscan evidence is to be found in the decorations of tombs excavated by archaeologists, a source of wonder even today. This detail of a fresco from a tomb at Tarquinii depicts Hades or Dis, as the Romans called him, king of the Underworld. He wears a wolf's head, to symbolize his omnivorous nature. The name Dis, like another Greek name for him, Pluto, means wealthy, showing the earth both as giver of wealth and receiver of an endless succession of the dead.

*Below*
Vulcan was the god of volcanic eruptions, well-known in Italy and Sicily from his periodic displays on Vesuvius and Etna. At his festival on 23rd August fish were fried alive, victims which would normally be safe in the sea from the god's power. He was identified with Hephaestus the Greek smith god who lived and worked beneath volcanos. In this picture by Ercole de Roberti, a sixteenth-century Ferra artist, he forges armour on his anvil with the aid of his assistants, the one-eyed Cyclopes. The two suits hanging above the workers' heads may perhaps be intended for Romulus and Remus, shown at right as infants still.

*Right*
As the patron of *mercatores* – merchants – Mercury made a comparatively late appearance on the Roman scene in 495 BC, when a temple was dedicated to him. The earlier Romans had been active in agriculture rather than in trade, and no doubt felt little need of such protection. Mercury was also Jupiter's messenger and portrayed with conveniently winged feet, as in this statue, in the Naples Museum. He had the same attributes as the Greek god Hermes, who was also worshipped by traders. Horace fancifully saw in the Emperor Augustus an incarnation of Mercury, young and engaging, the god of peaceful arts, restorer of economic prosperity to a world torn apart by civil war.

*Above*
This majestic figure of Ceres has ears of
corn in her hand, symbol of her authority
over agriculture. Her first temple at Rome
was dedicated after a famine in 496 BC.
The goddess, apparently, was imported
from Cumae, one of Rome's main corn
suppliers at that time. Her annual
festival — the Cerealia — was held for
eight days from 12th April. On its last
day foxes were let loose at the foot of
the Aventine Hill, where Ceres's temple
stood, with burning brands tied to their
tails. Ovid suggests that this
commemorated an occasion when a
fox caught stealing hens was wrapped
in straw to be burnt, then escaped,
burning the crops it ran through.
Scholars are much tested to explain
that one!

*Above right*
The Romans portrayed their gods as men,
so it was a small, albeit a significant, step
to regard certain men as divine. There
were precedents for this: Aeneas and
Romulus each had a divine parent, and
more recently Alexander the Great had
been venerated as a god among the
Greeks. Small wonder that the Romans
felt that Julius Caesar's tremendous
achievements warranted his apotheosis
after death. As Julius's adopted son,
Augustus claimed to be *divi filius* — son
of the divine — and after his death full
divine honours were paid to him and a
college of priests was established to
maintain his worship. This became the
custom with all but the most unpopular
emperors. In this statue from the Vatican
the Emperor Claudius is portrayed with

the eagle, symbol of Jupiter and Rome,
wearing a chaplet of oak leaves, in an
act of worship — a man and yet a god.

*Right*
The cult of Dionysus, latinized as Bacchus
arrived in Rome shortly after that of
Cybele (see page 60) and although
proscribed by the Senate, remained
popular. The God is usually shown as the
youthful god of wine and good living and
there are many representations of the
Bacchantes and their orgiastic rituals
involving large quantities of wine.
Women in particular seemed to indulge
in the crazy, drunken worship.

*Right*
Neptune was originally a not very important god of fresh water, who had nothing to do with salt water until the Romans identified him with the Greek Poseidon. The Romans themselves had little love of the sea, and avoided it wherever possible — witness the fact of the splendid road system throughout the Empire. Neptune's feast day was in midsummer on 23rd July, when streams were low and water scarce, a natural time for countrymen to appeal to a god of fresh water. His cult partner was Salacia, goddess of springing (*salire*) water. Once Neptune became identified with Poseidon, Roman poets assigned him the Greek god's adventures, and this mosaic from Tunisia also shows him in his Greek disguise.

*Below*
The process of deification was sometimes carried beyond the bounds of credulity. Antinous was the young favourite of the Emperor Hadrian, a rather melancholy and lonely man, as some of his surviving poetry shows. When his beloved Antinous was drowned in Egypt, Hadrian built a city and temples in his honour. Statues, set up elsewhere, emphasized his youth and beauty, as here, where the youth is portrayed as Bacchus with grapes in his hand and a carelessly worn leopard skin.

*Right*
This second-century temple to Hadrian at Ephesus is situated in a prominent part of the town, like many such temples built in honour of divine rulers throughout the Roman Empire. It was a matter of local pride to put up a worthy building and also a social honour to be elected to the college of priests who serviced it. There were commonly 15 priests, presided over by an ex-magistrate, and ceremonies were held on important anniversaries connected with the emperor concerned. All costs were borne locally, one of the reasons why Boudicca destroyed Colchester in the rebellion she led in East Anglia — Colchester was the site of a temple to Claudius.

# THE LEGENDS

CHAPTER

V

*Previous page*
Daphne, dedicated to virginity, successfully resisted the advances of all her suitors, although Peneus felt she owed him grandchildren. When she met Apollo, her beauty proved too much for that amorous god. She fled in terror from his embraces and begged her father to save her from Apollo's attentions by destroying her beauty. She was transformed on the spot into a laurel tree. Symbolizing her perpetual youth, the laurel is an evergreen, and ever after Apollo's brow was adorned with laurel leaves. Bernini has cleverly portrayed the moment of Daphne's transformation in this composition, which is now in Rome's Borghese Gallery.

*Right*
Ovid's stories of Jupiter's amorous escapades were a source of constant amusement to his contemporaries, particularly as the poet himself lived no cloistered life. One illustrated in this mosaic from a Cyprus villa built in the third century AD involved Ganymede, a pretty young shepherd of Troy. In order to carry Ganymede off to serve him as a cup-bearer — and as a constant irritation to Juno — Jupiter turned himself into an eagle, his own royal symbol. Other metamorphoses credited to the god are those of a fly, a swan, a bull and a shower of gold.

*Right*
Among Ovid's many poems, none is more charming than the 15 books of the *Metamorphoses*, or Transformations. In these books, legendary Greek and Roman heroes and heroines are transformed into various shapes and beings. One of Ovid's stories is that of the nymph Daphne, illustrated here with her father, the river god Peneus, in a mosaic pavement. Apollo had boasted that his hunting arrows were of more use than those of Cupid, which played havoc with people's affections. Cupid in anger shot Apollo with an arrow of passion and wounded Daphne, innocent victim, with another arrow which drove away all sexual desire.

*Far right*
Galatea, sea nymph and daughter of Nereus, a lesser god of the sea, lived off the coast of Sicily. As depicted here she attracted the attention of Polyphemus, one of the mythical one-eyed giants called the Cyclopes. Descendants of the original Sky and Earth, the Cyclopes were portrayed both as shepherds, like Polyphemus in this picture, and as blacksmiths at work in their forge under Mount Etna making thunderbolts for Jupiter. In the local legend the uncouth giant Polyphemus, in love with Galatea but rejected by her, transformed her handsome young lover Acis into a river by crushing him with a rock. The story, told by Ovid, is also the theme of one of Handel's operas.

*Right*
Many of the myths of Jupiter, which are largely those of the Greek Zeus, are preserved by Ovid. His *Fasti* tells how the constellation Capricorn got its name. As a baby on the island of Crete Jupiter was suckled along with Pan by a goat from the herd of a mountain nymph. The name Amalthea has been given variously both to the nymph and the goat. When one of the goat's horns fell off it was filled with fruit as a cornucopia, or horn of plenty, and presented to Jupiter by the nymph. The goat – *capra* – and the horn – *cornu* – were translated into stars. The same myth is depicted by Bernini in this small group from the Bernini Gallery.

*Below*
Narcissus was a handsome young man whose love for himself has immortalized his name in the textbooks of psychologists. One of his lovers prayed that as a punishment for his conceit and frigid disregard of those who loved him, Narcissus would fall desperately in love with someone unable to return his passion. When Narcissus saw his own reflection in a pool, as depicted in this mosaic, he fell so hopelessly in love with himself that he died of grief when his beloved appeared to avoid him. On his death he was transformed into the flower which bears his name.

*Right*
Ovid tells us that Medusa, a Gorgon, was once renowned for her beauty and roused jealous hopes in the hearts of many suitors. Most striking was her lovely hair. After Neptune seduced her in the Temple of Minerva, the goddess punished Medusa for her impiety by turning her hair into snakes. This is how Medusa is portrayed in this relief. She was slain by Perseus, who used her head to turn to stone all who looked at it. This magic talisman was worn as an effigy on Minerva's breastplate, and was a common feature on armour worn by Roman emperors.

# THE IMPORTS

## CHAPTER
## VI

*Previous pages*
The Romans usually tolerated and adapted foreign cults unless they were antisocial or subversive. Druidism, for example, was brutally put down in Britain and Gaul because its priests practised human sacrifice and encouraged rebellion against Roman power. Tolerance came from many years of experience and mistakes in Italy before they extended their empire. The worship of Magna Mater, the Great Mother, was frowned on at first by the Senate until it was seen to fulfil a spiritual, not a harmful, purpose. This tolerant attitude is illustrated by these statues of Neptune and Ceres at Smyrna in Turkey, which recall an unsavoury old myth of Neptune's seduction of Ceres, his sister.

*Above*
Cybele, the Great Mother, was a fertility goddess whose cult originated in Phrygia. It was traditionally brought to Rome in 204 BC, Livy tells us, at a critical point in the Second Punic War, following the advice given by the Sibylline Books. The ship bringing Cybele's statue from Phrygia stuck in the Tiber mud, but the sacred stone was passed from hand to hand by the women of Rome until it came to rest in the Temple of Victory on the Palatine. Cybele's male attendants were eunuchs and her worship was wild and orgiastic. Her annual festival, the Megalesia, on 4th April was strictly controlled by the puritanical Senate, who forbade Roman citizens to take part. This headless statue of the goddess, at Corinth, is a Roman work of the second century AD.

*Above right*
When the plague broke out in 293 BC, the Sibylline Books were consulted, before the embassy was sent to Delphi, and finally to Epidaurus. Here their reception was mixed. But Aesculapius appeared to one of their envoys in a dream and promised to come next day as a snake. This was a common epiphany of the god, as shown in this small Roman statue from a villa in Cyprus, where he holds a staff with a snake twined round it. The snake is phallic in appearance and therefore a symbol of life, and its venom also has medicinal qualities which were not unknown to the ancients.

The staff entwined by a snake is still the emblem commonly used by doctors to denote their profession.

*Right*
The sacred snake of Aesculapius obligingly boarded the ship which took the Roman embassy home from Epidaurus. As the ship was coming up the Tiber it slipped overboard and swam to the island which stands in midstream. Here a shrine was erected in Aesculapius's honour and this became a sanatorium, conveniently cut off by the water from the rest of the city. There is still a hospital here and a church, both dedicated to St Bartholomew, who has usurped the god's functions.

*Left*

The gods of Egypt were welcomed in Rome chiefly by the poorer classes, who probably enjoyed some of the more unsavoury aspects of their worship and the continual round of ritual, which was foreign to Roman ideas. The best-known gods were Isis and Osiris, rulers of the Underworld, the one representing the female reproductive force of nature, the other a legendary king murdered by his brother. When Egypt came under the control of Alexander the Great, his general Ptolemy introduced the god Serapis as a combination of Osiris and the Greek gods Zeus, Hades and Asclepius. Serapis was never popular with the Egyptians, but he was worshipped throughout the Roman Empire. This bust of him was found at the Roman colony of Carthage.

*Below left*

Ovid in his *Metamorphoses* tells how Aesculapius came to Rome. His name is a Latinized corruption of Asclepius, the legendary son of Apollo, patron of physicians, whom he helped by visiting the sick in their dreams. Centres of pilgrimage were to be found throughout the Greek-speaking world and the sick flocked to them in hopes of a cure. They spent their time lying on stretchers in the long colonnades which are a feature of such sanctuaries — this one is at Pergamum in Turkey. The most famous centre was at Epidaurus in Greece, where a Roman embassy came in 293 BC to ask Aesculapius to cure a pestilence that was raging in Rome.

*Top right*

Mithras was a god from Persia, and his first missionaries in the West were some pirates spared by Pompey the Great who settled in Italy. The religion was also spread by Roman troops who had served in the Eastern Mediterranean, and it always remained popular with soldiers. Unfortunately our knowledge of Mithraism is limited to what its opponents tell us and the interpretation of symbols never meant to be intelligible to outsiders. Mithras was apparently born from a rock and after various adventures caught and tamed a supernatural beast represented in sculpture as a large bull, which he afterwards sacrificed. This act is as central to Mithraism as the Crucifixion is to Christianity. This sculpture, now in the Vatican Museum, portrays the moment of sacrifice.

*Right*

Mithras was often identified with the sun and one of his commonest titles was Sol Invictus — the Unconquered Sun. His birthday fell on 25th December, so our Christmas has a Mithraic origin. In a meeting place such as this underground chamber, found under the Church of St Clement in Rome, devotees of Mithras underwent a series of seven grades of initiations which tested their courage and determination. A life of purity was the aim because Mithras stood for the triumph of good over evil.

ΚΑΛΛΙΟΠΗ       ΚΛΕΙω ΕΡΑΤω       ΜΕΛΠΟΜΕΝΗ

*Previous pages*
The Villa of the Mysteries at Pompeii
takes its name from the vivid series of
frescos in one of its rooms. An air of
religious mystery surrounds them, and
the various scenes have caused much
scholarly controversy. The central fresco
depicts the wedding of Bacchus and
Ariadne, presumably to symbolize the
physical bliss and mental satisfaction
which follow an initiation. Here a young
woman kneels with her head on an older
matron's lap while she is scourged,
perhaps to expiate the faults of her
previous life. The other scenes bear out
the interpretation that this is a Bacchic
mystery rite, which became so popular
in Italy as to be banned by decree of the
Senate in 186 BC.

ΧΟΡΗ   ΠΟΛΥΜΝΙΑ ΕΥΤΕΡΠΕΙ   ΘΑΛΕΙΑ ΟΥΡΑΝΙΑ

# THE SOURCES

## CHAPTER VII

Traditional sources of poetic inspiration were the nine Muses, here painted by the Sienese artist Baldassarre Peruzzi as attractive young women dancing with their patron and protector, Apollo. Their favourite mountain retreat was Parnassus, high above Delphi in Greece, site of Apollo's ancient oracle. Each Muse was responsible for a particular branch of the arts — Melpomene for tragedy, Calliope for epic, *inter alias*. Virgil opens his *Aeneid* with an invocation to one of them, a ritual copied from earlier Greek epic poets, and Ovid frequently mentions his need of their help. Even Livy ends the preface to his *History* with an appeal for divine assistance, which shows that Livy saw himself as a poet.

*Left*

In this mosaic portrait of Virgil, found in 1896 at Sousse in Tunisia, the poet is seated between two Muses, Melpomene clearly identified by the tragic mask in her hand, Clio, patroness of history, by the open scroll. The *Aeneid* on his knee is open at the words *Musa, mihi causas memora* – 'Muse, relate to me the reasons'.

Virgil died in his early fifties and was buried at Naples, where his tomb was revered in later ages. There is even a legend that St Paul wept at his grave. In his will Virgil directed that the *Aeneid* should be destroyed because it was imperfect. The Emperor Augustus fortunately prevented this, instructing the editors to correct and remove redundant passages but add nothing. The epitaph on Virgil's tomb contains his whole career in eleven Latin words:

Mantua gave me life, Calabria death –
    I lie
In Naples – poet of herdsmen, farms
    and heroes

*Below left*

Ovid was born in the Abruzzi, a mountainous region east of Rome whose isolation has only recently been penetrated by roads. Sulmona was Ovid's home town – *Sulmo mihi patria est* – a Latin phrase whose initial letters S M P E are now Sulmona's municipal motto. He came from a well-to-do but obscure family and was destined by education in Rome for a political career. But this proved uncongenial. In Pope's famous rendering, 'I lisped in numbers and the numbers came'; poetry was to be Ovid's life and he moved in a brilliant literary circle where he found much to his liking. This small town set high among the Apennines is typical of many in the district from which the poet came.

*Below*

In his fifties Ovid was banished from Rome to a barbaric frontier post, Tomi, later Constanza, in Rumania. The reasons are obscure, but his name was linked with that of Julia, the Emperor Augustus'

daughter, who had been banished earlier.
From Tomi Ovid poured out a series of
poems lamenting his fate, but to no
avail. The decree was never revoked, and
he died in exile. The modern Constanza
seems a pleasant place, and the Black Sea
coast has become a popular tourist centre.
But it was apparently very different in
Ovid's day, and he never ceased to
complain of the climate and his
surroundings. This statue of him was
erected at Constanza in 1879.

*Above*
Ovid wrote a quantity of poems, all with
a light touch, the majority in a racy and
humorous vein. One poem in 15 books of
hexameter verse is the *Metamorphoses*, a
rich store of mythology from the creation
of the world to the death of Julius Caesar.
The stories' common theme is, of course,
a change of shape. One such tale is that of
Venus's love for the handsome Adonis,
the subject of this voluptuous painting by
Veronese, now in the Prado in Madrid.
Ovid describes Adonis lying under a
poplar tree with his head resting on
Venus's breasts while she warned him
about the dangers of hunting. He
neglected her warning and was killed
by a wild boar – and anemones sprang
up where his blood had sprinkled
the ground.

ΘΙCΒΗ    ΠΥΡΑΜΟC

*Above*

Ovid's *Metamorphoses* has been used by writers as well as artists as a dictionary of mythology. Shakespeare read the poem at school and remembered many of the stories:

In such a night
Did Thisbe fearfully o'ertrip the dew,
And saw the lion's shadow ere himself,
And ran dismay'd away.

Jessica reminds Lorenzo in *The Merchant of Venice*. Pyramus and Thisbe, shown here in a mosaic from Cyprus, are also familiar from the brilliant and humorous scenes in *A Midsummer Night's Dream*, while Venus and Adonis are the subjects of a poem nearly 1200 lines long. The other work of Ovid's mature years is the *Fasti*, the Calendar. It is an account of the festivals in the Roman religious year, enlivened by much mythology. These two poems have provided much of the material for this book.

*Left*

Livy was born at Patavium in Northern Italy, which is now the flourishing modern city of Padua, seen here. He never lost his *patavinitas*, a feature of his Latin not always approved of by his contemporaries, and his bourgeois background is reflected in his detachment from the political struggles of his time. His history of Rome from its foundation to his own day comprised 142 books, most of which have been lost. Enough survives to appreciate the value of Livy's work, and some of his material has been used here to relate the stories of early Rome. Unashamedly patriotic, even in the face of facts, Livy sees this early period as the reason for Rome's greatness in his own time. He may not measure up to what we expect of a historian today, but as a storyteller he is unforgettable.

*Right*

The Golden Age of Latin literature, when Livy, Ovid and Virgil were all writing, was presided over by the Emperor Augustus, here shown in Olympian pose with an infant Rome at his feet. This flowering of literature was no accident but the result of Augustus' deliberate policy, and carried out by his friend Maecenas, who gathered around him a circle of writers. In days when the sale of books was no means of livelihood, patronage was a professional writer's only hope. Certainly Augustus took a close personal interest in literature — we are told that Virgil read many passages of the *Aeneid* to him. So the patriotic sentiments should hardly surprise us.

MVNIF·PI·IX·P·M·
AN·XVIII

On Mount Parnassus, Apollo, patron of the arts, sits under the laurel trees sacred to him, playing his lyre. He is surrounded by the figures of all nine Muses and many writers, prominent among them the three great poets of Greek, Latin and Italian literature, Homer, Virgil and Dante, who stand on the left of Apollo. This delightful combination of fact and fancy was painted by Raphael as one of a series of frescoes in the Vatican. Perhaps better than any other, this picture summarizes the influence of classical mythology and of the writers who have made it a tradition that is still living today.